Letts

GCSE IN A WEEK

ADDITIONAL SCIENCE

Hannah Kingston
Emma Poole
Caroline Reynolds

Revision Planner

Page	Day	Time (mins)	Title	Exam Board	Date	Time	Completed
4	1	15 mins	How Science Works	AEO			

Biology

Page	Day	Time (mins)	Title	Exam Board	Date	Time	Completed
6	1	10 mins	Cells	AEO			
8	1	15 mins	Diffusion and Osmosis	AO			
10	1	15 mins	Enzymes and Nutrition	OA			
12	1	15 mins	The Environment	AO, E (except Pyramids)			
14	1	10 mins	Interactions in Environments	E			
16	1	15 mins	Cycles	AEO			
18	1	15 mins	Respiration and Exercise	E, AO (except Exercise)			
20	1	15 mins	Homeostasis	A			
22	2	15 mins	Excretion and Homeostasis	A			
24	2	15 mins	Mitosis	AEO			
26	2	15 mins	Meiosis	AEO			
28	2	15 mins	Genes	AO (except Protein Synthesis) E			
30	2	15 mins	Manipulating Life	EO			
32	2	15 mins	Inheritance and Disease	A			
34	2	10 mins	Food Production	EO			
36	2	10 mins	Plant Hormones	AEO			
38	3	15 mins	Plant Growth	AEO			
40	3	15 mins	Animal Growth	EO			
42	3	15 mins	The Circulatory System	O			

Chemistry

Page	Day	Time (mins)	Title	Exam Board	Date	Time	Completed
44	3	15 mins	Atomic Structure	AEO			
46	3	15 mins	Electronic Structure	AEO			
48	3	15 mins	Ionic Bonding	AEO			
50	3	15 mins	Covalent Bonding	AEO			
52	3	15 mins	Alkali Metals	AEO			
54	4	15 mins	Noble Gases and Halogens	AEO			
56	4	15 mins	Calculations	AEO			
58	4	15 mins	Haber Process	AEO			
60	4	15 mins	Rates of Reaction	AE			

Page	Day	Time (mins)	Title	Exam Board	Date	Time	Completed

Chemistry cont...

Page	Day	Time (mins)	Title	Exam Board	Date	Time	Completed
62	4	15 mins	Energy	AE			
64	4	15 mins	Aluminium	O			
66	4	15 mins	Sodium Chloride	AEO			
68	4	15 mins	Making Salts	AO			
70	5	15 mins	Metals	AEO			
72	5	15 mins	Water	O			
74	5	15 mins	Detergents	O			
76	5	15 mins	Special Materials	AEO			
78	5	15 mins	Vegetable Oils	E			
80	5	15 mins	Alkanes and Alkenes	AEO			
82	5	15 mins	Polymers	E			

Physics

Page	Day	Time (mins)	Title	Exam Board	Date	Time	Completed
84	6	15 mins	Motion	AEO			
86	6	15 mins	Graphs for Motion	AEO			
88	6	15 mins	When Forces Combine	AEO			
90	6	15 mins	Forces and Motion	AEO			
92	6	15 mins	Momentum and Stopping	AEO			
94	6	15 mins	Safe Driving	AEO			
96	6	15 mins	Energy and Work	AEO			
98	6	15 mins	Work and Power	AEO			
100	6	15 mins	Inside the Atom	AEO			
102	7	15 mins	Radiation and Science	AEO			
104	7	15 mins	Safe Radiation	AEO			
106	7	15 mins	Nuclear Power	AEO			
108	7	15 mins	Radiation Issues	EO			
110	7	15 mins	Static Electricity	AEO			
112	7	15 mins	Electricity on the Move 1	AO			
114	7	15 mins	Electricity on the Move 2	AO			
116	7	15 mins	Using Electricity	AO			
118	7	15 mins	Waves	AO			

How Science Works

Understanding scientific ideas helps us to plan and carry out experiments and become better citizens.

Ideas

Sometimes our opinions are based on our own prejudices – what we personally like or dislike. At other times, our opinions can be based on scientific evidence. These opinions are based on reliable and valid evidence that can be used to back up our opinion.

Variables

- An **independent** variable is the variable that we choose to change to see what happens.

- A **dependent** variable is the variable that we measure.

- A **continuous** variable, e.g. time or mass, can have any numerical value.

- An **ordered** variable, e.g. small, medium or large, can be listed in order.

- A **discrete** variable can have any value which is a whole number, e.g. 1, 2.

- A **categoric** variable is a variable that can be labelled, e.g. red, blue.

- We use **line graphs** to present data where the independent variable and the dependent variable are both continuous. A line of best fit can be used to show the relationship between variables.

- **Bar graphs** are used to present data when the independent variable is categoric and the dependent variable is continuous.

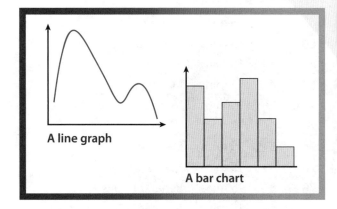

A line graph

A bar chart

Evidence

Evidence should be:

- **reliable** (if you do it again you get the same result)

- **accurate** (close to the true value).

Scientists often try to find links between variables.

Links can be:

- causal – a change in one variable produces a change in the other variable

- a chance occurrence

- due to an association, where both of the observed variables are linked by a third variable.

We can use our existing models and ideas to suggest why something happens. This is called a **hypothesis**. We can use this hypothesis to make a **prediction** that can be tested. When the data is collected, if it does not back up our original models and ideas we need to check that the data is valid, and if it is we need to go back and change our original models and ideas.

Science in Society

Sometimes scientists investigate subjects that have social consequences, e.g. food safety. When this happens, decisions may be based on a combination of the evidence and other factors, such as bias or political considerations.

Although science is helping us to understand more about our world there are still some questions that we cannot answer, such as: Is there life on other planets? Some questions are for everyone in society to answer, not just scientists, such as: should we clone people?

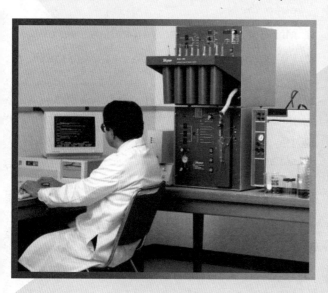

PROGRESS CHECK

1. What is an independent variable?

2. What is a dependent variable?

3. What is an ordered variable?

4. What is a discrete variable?

5. What does accurate mean?

? EXAM QUESTION

A student carries out an experiment to find out how the force applied to a spring affects the length of the spring.

a. What is the independent variable?

b. What is the dependent variable?

c. Suggest a variable that must be controlled to make it a fair test.

Cells

Cells are the building blocks of life. All living things are made up of cells.

Animal and Plant Cells

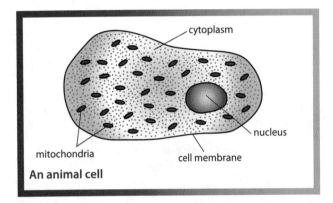

An animal cell

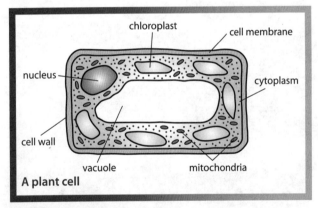

A plant cell

Animal and plant cells have:	Only plant cells have:
a nucleus cytoplasm a cell membrane mitochondria ribosomes	a cell wall a vacuole chloroplasts

Parts of Animal and Plant Cells

■ The **nucleus** controls all the chemical reactions that take place inside the cell. The nucleus also contains **all the information** needed to produce a new living organism.

■ The **cytoplasm** is where the **chemical reactions** take place. Chemical reactions are controlled by enzymes.

■ The **cell membrane** controls what passes **in and out** of the cell.

■ **Mitochondria** are where **respiration** takes place.

■ **Ribosomes** are in the cytoplasm and are the site of protein synthesis.

■ The **cell wall** is made of **cellulose**, which gives a plant cell **strength and support**.

■ The **vacuole** contains a weak solution of salt and sugar called **cell sap**. The vacuole also gives the cell support.

■ **Chloroplasts** contain a substance called **chlorophyll** to absorb the Sun's energy so that the plant can **photosynthesise**.

Special Cells

Cells are different shapes in order to carry out particular functions more efficiently.

Specialised Animal Cells

A **sperm cell** has a **tail** to help it to swim towards the egg. Its head is streamlined to aid swimming.

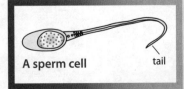

A sperm cell   tail

Red blood cells have **no nucleus** so there is more room for oxygen. They are also **biconcave** for maximum surface area.

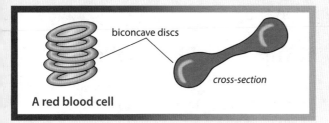

biconcave discs

cross-section

A red blood cell

Specialised Plant Cells

Root hair cells are **long and thin** to absorb water and minerals from the soil.

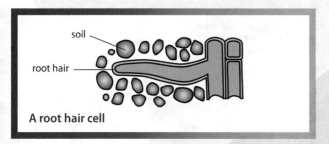

soil

root hair

A root hair cell

Palisade cells have **many chloroplasts**. These cells are near the upper surface of the leaf so the chloroplasts can absorb sunlight for photosynthesis.

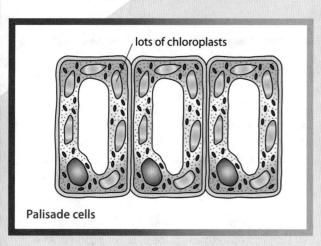

lots of chloroplasts

Palisade cells

Stem Cell Therapy

Stem cells are cells that have the ability to replicate and specialise into different types of tissue throughout the life of the organism. They are found in adult bone marrow, the brain, blood and heart, human embryos and the umbilical cord. Embryonic stem cells have the ability to divide and specialise into any tissue needed, such as nerve cells.

Stem cells from adults do not have the same ability to change into any type of cell; they can only change into a cell from where they originated. These stem cells are also scarce in the body and harder to culture.

The potential for stem cell therapy is endless. They can be used to replace tissue that has lost its function, such as damaged heart tissue, and used to treat genetic diseases.

In the future, stem cells could be used to treat burn victims, spinal cord injuries, heart disease, cancer and diabetes. It could mean the end of mechanical devices such as artificial joints and plastic arteries by using living, natural replacements.

PROGRESS CHECK

1. What occurs in the mitochondria?
2. What is a specialised cell?
3. What are stem cells?

EXAM QUESTION

1. Plant cells have different structures from animal cells. Which of the following features do only plant cells have?

   chloroplast   nucleus   cell wall

2. What is the function of the chloroplasts?

Diffusion and Osmosis

Living things move substances around by diffusion and osmosis.

Simple Diffusion

Diffusion is **the movement of particles from an area of high concentration to an area of low concentration until they are evenly spread out.**

Rules to Remember

Diffusion occurs at a faster rate if:

- the particle size is smaller
- the diffusion distance is smaller
- the surface area for diffusion is increased
- the difference in concentration is large. (This is called a **concentration gradient.**)

Diffusion in Animal Cells

For respiration, glucose diffuses into the blood from the small intestine and oxygen diffuses into the blood from the alveoli in the lungs. They are carried in the blood to the cells where they diffuse into the cell.

Diffusion occurs during the exchange of carbon dioxide and oxygen in the alveoli of the lungs.

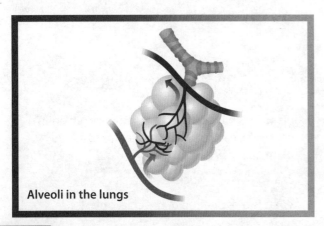

Alveoli in the lungs

Diffusion in Plant Cells

During photosynthesis, carbon dioxide diffuses into the leaf via the stomata (holes) found on the underside of a leaf.

Oxygen and water vapour diffuse out of the stomata, particularly in hot, dry, windy conditions.

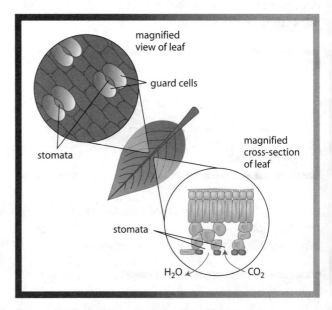

magnified view of leaf

guard cells

magnified cross-section of leaf

stomata

stomata

H_2O CO_2

Adaptations for Diffusion

There are millions of thin-walled alveoli in the lungs so they present a large surface area. They are in very close contact with lots of blood capillaries (which means there is a short diffusion distance). Blood is continually taking away oxygen, which sets up a concentration gradient.

The inner surface of the small intestine contains many villi that increase the surface area for absorption of food molecules by diffusion into the blood. The villi also have a good blood supply.

Osmosis

Osmosis is **the movement of water molecules from an area of high water concentration (weak/dilute solution) to an area of low water concentration (strong/concentrated solution) through a partially permeable membrane.**

'Partially permeable' means it allows small molecules to pass through but not larger ones.

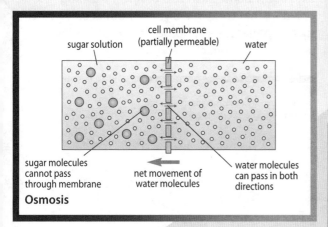

Osmosis

Osmosis in Plant Cells

Root hairs take in water from the soil by **osmosis**. Water continues to move along the cells of the root and up the xylem to the leaf. Osmosis makes plant cells swell up. The water moves into the plant cell vacuole and pushes against the cell wall. The cell wall stops the cell from bursting. We say that the cell is **turgid**. This is useful as it gives plant stems support.

If a plant is lacking in water then it wilts and the cells become **flaccid** as water moves out of the cells. If a lot of water leaves the cells then the cytoplasm starts to peel away from the cell walls. The cells have undergone **plasmolysis**.

Osmosis in Animal Cells

Animal cells have no cell wall to stop them swelling, so if they are placed in pure water, they take in water by osmosis until they burst!

PROGRESS CHECK

1. What is diffusion?

2. What substance moves by osmosis?

3. Why do animal cells burst if they are placed in pure water?

EXAM QUESTION

1. Diffusion occurs in animal and plant cells. Give one example of diffusion in:

   a. plant cells

   b. animal cells.

2. Describe and explain how the features of alveoli in the lungs make them efficient at diffusion.

Enzymes and Nutrition

Enzymes act as biological catalysts by speeding up chemical reactions.

What are Enzymes?

Enzymes are proteins made up of long chains of amino acids. Each enzyme has its own number and sequence of amino acids resulting in specific functions.

An enzyme is folded into a specific shape that allows other molecules, called substrates, to fit into its **active site**. The enzyme and the substrate fit together using a **lock and key** mechanism. Enzymes are highly specific to substrates.

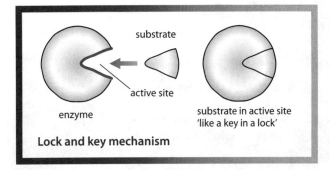

Lock and key mechanism

Enzymes are called **biological catalysts**. They speed up or catalyse biological reactions inside cells such as respiration, protein synthesis and photosynthesis. Enzyme activity is affected by pH and temperature. Each enzyme has its own **optimum** conditions, e.g. pepsin in the stomach works in low pH conditions.

Enzymes in the human body work best at 37 °C, which is our normal body temperature. At too low temperatures, the rate at which the substrate joins with the enzyme's active site is slowed down so the reaction is slower. At too high temperatures or extremes of pH, the enzyme becomes denatured and the reaction stops. This is an irreversible change because the active site is distorted.

Uses of Enzymes in the Home and Industry

Enzymes are cheap to use in industry and the home as they do not need high temperatures to work and can be reused.

Uses in the home include **biological washing powders** that contain enzymes produced by bacteria, such as proteases and lipases to digest fats and protein stains from clothes.

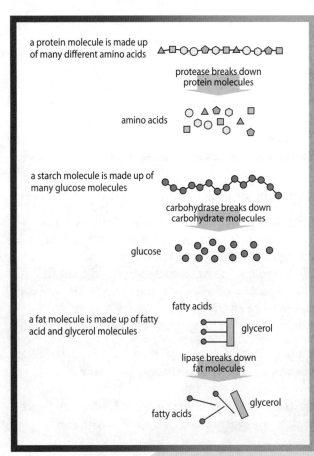

In **industry**, carbohdrases are used in the making of chocolate and syrup. Proteases are used to pre-digest the protein in baby food. Isomerase is used to convert glucose syrup into the much sweeter fructose syrup. This is used in smaller quantities in slimming foods.

Digestion and Enzymes

Digestion is the breaking down of **large insoluble** molecules into **small soluble** molecules so that they can be absorbed into the bloodstream. This action is speeded up (catalysed) by **enzymes**. Enzymes are found throughout the digestive system and work outside the body cells.

Starch, protein and fats are large, insoluble molecules.

- Starch is broken down into glucose in the mouth and small intestine by carbohydrase enzymes.

- Proteins are broken down into amino acids in the stomach and the small intestine by protease enzymes.

- Fats are broken down into fatty acids and glycerol in the small intestine by lipase enzymes

PROGRESS CHECK

1. What factors affect how enzymes work?

2. Give an example of how proteases are used in industry.

3. What type of enzymes break down starch in the body?

? EXAM QUESTION

In the body, hydrogen peroxide is broken down into oxygen and water by an enzyme called catalase.

Raw liver and fresh potato contain enzymes. In an experiment they were each added to test tubes of hydrogen peroxide and the amount of bubbles of oxygen released were counted. The liver produced more oxygen bubbles in 10 minutes than the potato.

a. Why was it important to use the same size cubes of potato and liver?

b. Suggest why the liver was more effective at breaking down the hydrogen peroxide.

The Environment

The ultimate source of energy in the environment is the energy from sunlight that is harnessed by green plants in photosynthesis.

Pyramid of Numbers

If we look at the information in a food chain or food web, it simply shows us who eats who or what. A pyramid of numbers, however, shows us how many organisms are involved at each stage in a food chain. At each level of a food chain (trophic level) the number of organisms *generally* gets less.

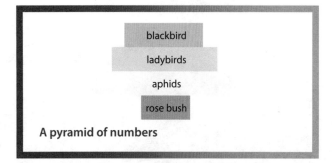

A pyramid of numbers

Sometimes a pyramid of numbers does not look like a pyramid at all as the mass of the organisms is not taken into account.

Pyramids of Biomass

A pyramid of biomass takes into account the **mass** *and* **numbers of organisms** in a food chain.

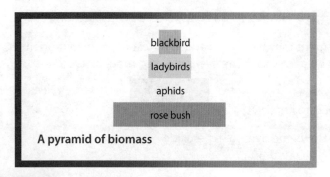

A pyramid of biomass

Loss of Energy

Food chains rarely have more than four or five links. The final organism is only getting a fraction of the energy that was produced at the beginning of the food chain.

Plants absorb their energy from the Sun. Only a small fraction of this energy is converted into glucose during photosynthesis. Some energy is lost to decomposers as plants shed their leaves, seeds or fruit. The plant uses some energy during respiration and growth. The plant's biomass (size) increases, which provides food for the herbivores.

At the primary consumer level, energy losses include waste products and energy used to keep warm.

Photosynthesis

Photosynthesis is a chemical process that plants use to make glucose.

The leaf is the **organ of photosynthesis**. It makes all the food (glucose) for the plant. A plant stores some of this glucose as starch and the rest is converted into useful substances that the plant needs.

The word equation of photosynthesis is:

$$\text{carbon dioxide} + \text{water} \xrightarrow[\text{chlorophyll}]{\text{light}} \text{glucose} + \text{oxygen}$$

The leaf has many features that enable it to carry out photosynthesis efficiently.

Leaves:

■ are **flat** with a **large surface area** to absorb sunlight

■ are **thin** so carbon dioxide can reach the inner cells easily

■ have **plenty of stomata** in the lower surface for gas exchange by diffusion

■ have **plenty of veins** to support the leaf and carry substances to and from all the cells in the leaf and plant

■ contain chlorophyll to absorb light.

Factors Affecting the Rate of Photosynthesis

There are *three* things that affect the rate of photosynthesis. We call them **limiting factors:**

■ amount of light

■ amount of carbon dioxide

■ temperature.

We can measure the rate of photosynthesis by how much oxygen is produced in a given time.

At any given time, any one of these factors could be limiting the rate of photosynthesis. Usually the rate of photosynthesis is limited by the temperature being too low as is the case for plants not normally grown in Britain.

Greenhouses help maintain a high enough temperature for optimum growth conditions – the amount of carbon dioxide and light can be maximised too.

PROGRESS CHECK

1. What type of pyramid takes into account the number of organisms in a food chain?

2. What type of pyramid takes into account the number *and* mass of organisms?

3. What are limiting factors?

? EXAM QUESTION

1. Copy and complete the word equation for photosynthesis:

a. _____ + water $\xrightarrow[\text{chlorophyll}]{\text{light}}$ b. _____ + oxygen

2. What **three** factors affect the rate of photosynthesis?

3. How have leaves adapted for photosynthesis?

Interactions in Environments

Living organisms interact in an environment and have an effect on the environment itself.

Human Activity

Human activity is affecting the environment all over the world. More people are using up more resources with more intensity than at any point in human history.

Problems caused include:

- **Deforestation** – the chopping down of trees and the failure to replace them. Deforestation can destroy habitats and increase the level of carbon dioxide in the air. This contributes to global warming and the greenhouse effect.

- **Pollution** – the growth of industrialisation has meant using up vast amounts of non-renewable fossil fuels. Burning fossil fuels releases gases that contribute to the greenhouse effect, pollution and acid rain.

There are animals and plants called **indicator species** that indicate pollution by their absence or presence. Lichens (a plant/fungus association) for example, are found on the bark of trees and other areas like gravestones. Certain species of lichen are very susceptible to pollution and die if pollution is too high.

In intensive farming, the use of fertilisers causes **eutrophication** in rivers and streams.

People around the world can have different impacts on the environment depending on their **economic** and **industrial** conditions.

Interdependence

Organisms in an environment interact and rely on each other for life; we say they are **interdependent**. A food web shows the interdependence of organisms with each other. Factors such as over-fishing of North Sea cod will affect aquatic food webs.

Animals and plants adapt to where they live in order to survive; they compete with each other for resources and are under threat from predators and disease. These factors and interactions between animals, plants and their environment affect population numbers and distribution in a community.

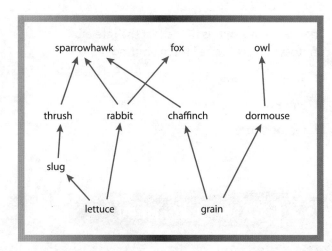

Extreme Environments

In extreme environments, the conditions determine what animals and plants exist and survive. Deep sea volcanic vents were only discovered in 1977. They are regions on the ocean floor where fluids and gases like methane and hydrogen sulfide (that smells like rotten eggs) seep through from the Earth's crust. They occur along the mid ocean ridge. These fluids and gases are so far down in the ocean that there is no light for photosynthetic organisms to survive.

Food webs do exist in these conditions though. The primary producers are bacteria that use energy from hydrogen sulfide and oxygen to make food, which is then used by other organisms. Because they are using chemicals and not light to obtain energy the process is called **chemosynthesis**.

Proteins in the bacteria are able to withstand the extremely high temperatures (up to 400 °C); they are resistant to the heat.

Other extreme environments that promote adaptations to survive are the Antarctic, where animals have had to adapt to the extreme cold, and high altitudes where there is a lack of oxygen.

PROGRESS CHECK

1. What does the term 'interdependence' mean?

2. What are indicator species used for?

3. What is deforestation?

EXAM QUESTION

Deep sea volcanic vents are regions of ocean floor where there is no light and only gases such as methane and hydrogen sulfide exist.

a. Describe how organisms such as bacteria survive in these vents.

b. Name **two** other extreme environments.

c. What is the difference between photosynthesis and chemosynthesis?

Cycles

Substances like carbon, nitrogen and water cycle naturally within the environment.

The Carbon Cycle

Carbon dioxide is a rare atmospheric gas; it makes up approximately 0.03% of the atmosphere. The amount of carbon released into the atmosphere balances the amount absorbed by plants.

Photosynthesis

■ Plants absorb carbon dioxide from the air.

■ They use the carbon to make carbohydrates, proteins and fats using the **Sun** as an energy source.

Feeding

■ Animals eat plants and take the carbon into their bodies to make up their carbohydrates, fats and proteins.

Respiration

■ Plants, animals and decomposers respire.

■ Respiration releases carbon dioxide back into the atmosphere.

Death and Decay

■ Plants and animals die and produce waste. The carbon is released into the soil.

Decomposers

■ Bacteria and fungi (also known as saprophytes) present in the soil are decomposers that break down dead matter, urine and faeces, which contain carbon. The ideal conditions for decomposition are **warmth**, **moisture** and **oxygen**. Without these factors, decay and decomposition cannot take place.

Death but no Decay

■ Plants and animals die but do not decay.

■ Heat and pressure gradually, over millions of years, produce fossil fuels containing carbon.

Fossil Fuels

■ Coal is formed from plants; oil and gas are produced from animals.

Burning and Combustion

■ The burning of fossil fuels (coal, oil and gas) releases carbon dioxide into the atmosphere.

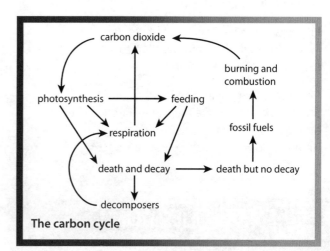

The carbon cycle

The Nitrogen Cycle

The atmosphere contains 78% nitrogen gas. Nitrogen is an important element needed for making **proteins**. Plants and animals cannot use nitrogen in this form. It has to be **converted to nitrates** before plants can use it to make protein.

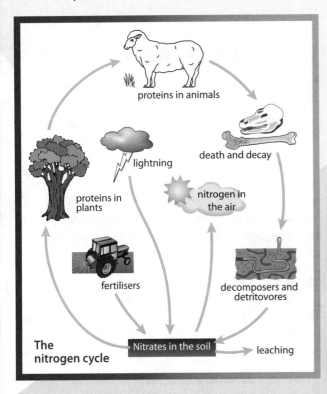

The nitrogen cycle

- Nitrogen is in the air.
- **Lightning** causes nitrogen and oxygen to combine to form nitrogen oxides. These dissolve in rain and are washed into the soil to form **nitrates** in the soil.
- Fertilisers can be added to the soil to improve the **nitrate** content.
- **Nitrogen-fixing bacteria** in the soil and roots of some plants convert nitrogen from the air into **nitrates**.

- Plants take up the **nitrates** from the soil and convert them into **proteins**.
- Animals eat the plants **and incorporate the protein i**nto their bodies.
- Animals and plants produce waste; they eventually die and their bodies decay. **Decomposers** such as fungi and bacteria turn this material into ammonium compounds that contain nitrogen.
- **Nitrifying bacteria** in the soil change **ammonia into nitrates**.
- **Nitrates** can be washed out of the soil before plants take them up. This is called **leaching** and can have serious consequences for rivers and streams.
- **Denitrifying bacteria** live in waterlogged soils; they can change nitrates back into ammonia and nitrogen gas that is returned to the atmosphere.

PROGRESS CHECK

1. Name the process that absorbs carbon dioxide from the air.

2. What are the **two** ways that carbon is released back into the air?

3. What do plants need nitrates for?

EXAM QUESTION

1. Name the **three** types of bacteria involved in the nitrogen cycle.

2. Explain their roles in the nitrogen cycle.

Respiration and Exercise

Respiration supplies the body with energy for various processes, including exercise.

Aerobic Respiration

Respiration is the **breakdown of glucose to make energy using oxygen**.

Aerobic means 'with air' and as respiration needs oxygen, we call it **aerobic respiration**.

During exercise, breathing and pulse rates increase. The arteries supplying the muscles also dilate. This delivers oxygen and glucose more quickly to the respiring muscles and removes carbon dioxide via the blood.

The word equation for respiration is:

glucose + oxygen ➜ carbon dioxide + water + **ENERGY**

Anaerobic Respiration

During strenuous exercise, oxygen supply is insufficient to meet the demands of the body, but energy is still needed. Respiration **without oxygen** is called **anaerobic respiration**. It produces **much less energy** and doesn't break down glucose completely.

This is the word equation:

glucose ➜ lactic acid + **ENERGY**

Instead of carbon dioxide, **lactic acid** is produced. It builds up in muscles and causes them to ache and cramp (contract spasmodically). Fast, deep breathing as you recover soon supplies the body with enough oxygen to combine with the lactic acid and convert it to carbon dioxide and water. An increase in heart rate ensures the blood carries lactic acid away to the liver where it is broken down when oxygen becomes available. The amount of oxygen needed to oxidise the lactic acid to carbon dioxide and water is called the **oxygen debt**.

Exercise and Fitness

During exercise, an increase in heart rate and breathing rate is normal, but just how much they increase during and after exercise can indicate a person's fitness.

A way to measure fitness could be to look at how long it takes for a person's pulse rate to return to normal after exercise. This is known as the **recovery rate**. You take a pulse rate before exercise (resting rate). Take it for 15 seconds, then multiply by 4 to get the number of beats per minute.

The best place to take a reading is on the carotid artery in the neck or the radial artery on the underside of the wrist. Then, exercise. Take the pulse again immediately after exercise and then every minute until the pulse returns to resting rate.

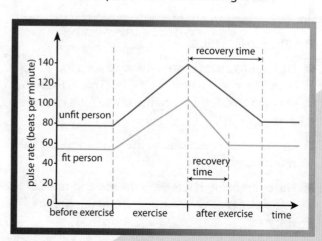

A fit person will recover much more quickly than an unfit person; an unfit person is also more likely to have a higher pulse rate before, during and after exercise.

Breathing rate and heart rate monitors can be worn on the wrist or around the body by the heart; they are a far more accurate way of taking measurements than by hand because they produce a continuous measurement before, during and after exercise. There is also less chance of human error in the readings.

PROGRESS CHECK

1. Define aerobic respiration.

2. Define anaerobic respiration.

3. What is the 'oxygen debt'?

? EXAM QUESTION

Look at the table. It shows the pulse rate in beats per minute of two athletes before, immediately after exercise, and then after a further 5 minutes.

Athlete	Pulse rate in beats per min		
	Before	After	After 5 minutes
A	70	135	70
B	75	140	90

a. Which athlete was fitter?

b. How could you tell from the results?

c. What would be the most accurate way to measure pulse rate and why?

Homeostasis

The nervous system and hormones enable us to respond to **external** changes in the environment and monitor and change our **internal** environment so that conditions stay at safe levels. This is called **homeostasis**.

Hormonal effects tend to be slower, long lasting and can affect a number of organs. Nervous control is much quicker, doesn't last very long and is confined to one area.

Internal conditions of the body that are controlled include:

- water content
- ion content
- temperature
- blood sugar levels.

blood glucose level normal → liver and pancreas sense blood glucose level too high → blood sugar level normal → liver takes up extra glucose from the blood → pancreas secretes insulin → pancreas stops secreting insulin and secretes glucagon → liver releases glucose into the blood → blood glucose level normal

Negative feedback

Diabetes

The pancreas maintains the level of glucose (sugar) in the blood so that there is enough for respiration. Diabetes results when the **pancreas** doesn't make enough of the **hormone insulin**.

Diabetes can be controlled by **attention to diet** – a low glucose diet can be all that is needed. In more severe cases, diabetics have to **inject** themselves with **insulin** before meals.

The pancreas secretes two hormones: **insulin and glucagon**. The liver responds to insulin, takes up excess glucose and stores it as **glycogen**.

Glucagon stimulates the conversion of stored glycogen in the liver back into glucose. This is an example of **negative feedback**.

Scientists Banting and Best discovered the link between insulin and diabetes late in the 19th century.

Manipulating Genes

Genetic engineering has been used to treat people with diabetes by the production of the protein, insulin. In brief:

- The gene that codes for insulin can be found in human pancreas cells.

- It is extracted from the chromosome and transplanted into a bacterium.

- The bacterium multiplies in a fermentation vessel and produces insulin.

- The insulin is removed and used to treat diabetes.

Body Temperature

Warm-blooded animals have mechanisms that can keep body temperature constant. The hypothalamus in the brain has receptors sensitive to the temperature of the blood flowing through it. The skin also has receptors that send impulses to the brain giving information about skin temperature. Inside your body the temperature stays around the same at **37 °C**.

When it's hot:

- blood vessels at the surface of the skin **widen** (called **vasodilation**) allowing more blood to flow to the surface

- heat **radiates** from the skin and is lost

- sweat glands secrete sweat

- the sweat **evaporates** from the skin and takes away **heat energy**.

When it's cold:

- blood vessels at the surface of the skin **contract** (called **vasoconstriction**) so that very little blood reaches the surface

- very little heat is lost by radiation

- muscles contract quickly (shivering) which produces extra heat

- sweat glands stop producing sweat

- increased respiration helps generate heat, as does exercise.

Many warm-blooded animals have a thick layer of fat beneath their skin for insulation.

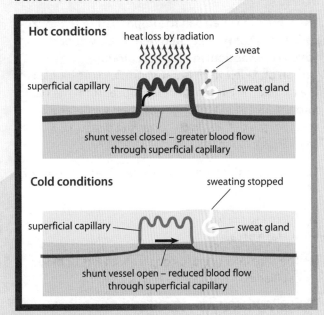

PROGRESS CHECK

1. What is homeostasis?

2. What causes diabetes?

3. Where is insulin made in the body?

EXAM QUESTION

Tom was walking outside in the cold; he looked pale and was shivering.

a. Explain how his body was working to try to keep him warm.

b. Which part of the brain monitors body temperature?

c. At which temperature is our body maintained? Choose the correct answer:

    37 °C   40 °C   35 °C

Excretion and Homeostasis

Excretion is the removal of toxic waste products from the body. It is controlled by various organs. Homeostasis is the mechanism by which the body **maintains a constant internal environment**.

The Lungs

The lungs are situated in the upper part of the torso called the **thorax**, separated from the lower part, which is the **abdomen**. Our cells produce waste carbon dioxide, which is transported to the lungs by the blood. The carbon dioxide diffuses from the blood into the alveoli in the lungs and then we breathe it out. Oxygen diffuses in the opposite direction. This is called **gas exchange**.

The alveoli in the lungs are well designed for their job of gas exchange.

- There are millions of them that present a **large surface area**.

- They are in **very close contact** with lots of blood capillaries.

- Their surface lining is moist so the gases can dissolve before they diffuse across the **thin membrane**.

	Intercostal muscles	Ribs	Diaphragm	Volume of chest
Breathing in	contract	move up and out	contracts and moves down	increases
Breathing out	relax	move down and in	relaxes and moves up	decreases

Composition of Gases

Gas	Inhaled air (%)	Exhaled air (%)
oxygen	21	16
carbon dioxide	0.04	4
nitrogen	79	79
water vapour	varies	high

The Kidney

The kidney has a major role in homeostasis as it controls the amount of water in our body (**osmoregulation**) and the removal of excess substances and the poisonous urea (**excretion**).

Urea is produced in the liver from excess amino acids. Various salts (ions) are taken into the body in food and absorbed into the blood; any excess salts are removed by the kidneys and in sweat. Water regulation is monitored by the pituitary gland in the brain, which releases a hormone called ADH. The kidneys and ADH balance water gain with water loss.

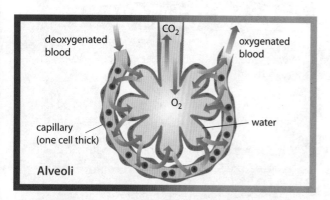

deoxygenated blood

CO_2

oxygenated blood

O_2

capillary (one cell thick)

water

Alveoli

Breathing in and out is called **ventilation**. Two sets of intercostal muscles between the ribs and the diaphragm help us breathe.

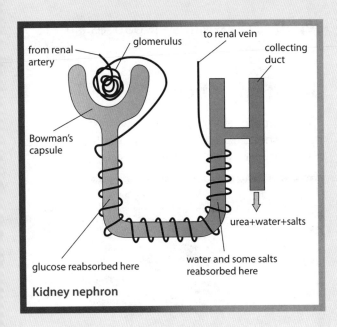

from renal artery
glomerulus
to renal vein
collecting duct
Bowman's capsule
urea+water+salts
glucose reabsorbed here
water and some salts reabsorbed here

Kidney nephron

Liquid in the **nephron** contains useful substances like glucose and some ions. These must be **reabsorbed**.

As the blood enters the first coiled tubule, useful substances are **reabsorbed** by **active transport** using **energy**. Reabsorption continues in the second coiled tubule.

The cleaned blood enters the renal vein and leaves the kidney. All urea and excess ions and water pass from the tubule into the collecting duct. This fluid continues out of the kidney into the ureter and down to the bladder as **urine**.

The amount of water that is reabsorbed depends on a hormone called **ADH** (antidiuretic hormone). ADH is released when more water needs to be reabsorbed – the result is more concentrated urine.

Ultrafiltration

The blood arrives in the **renal artery** at **high pressure** and enters the group of capillaries called the **glomerulus**.

High pressure squeezes water, urea, ions and glucose out of the blood into the **Bowman's capsule**. Large molecules stay in the blood.

? EXAM QUESTION

Urea is a toxic substance that needs to be removed from the body in urine.

a. Where is urea formed in the body and from what substance?

b. Explain how the kidneys remove urea from the body.

c. What other substances make up urine?

👁 PROGRESS CHECK

1. What is gas exchange?

2. How have alveoli adapted for efficient gas exchange?

3. What is osmoregulation?

Mitosis

Mitosis occurs in **growth**, **replacement** and **repair** of cells. Mitosis produces all cells except the sex cells, which are formed by meiosis.

In mitosis, a cell divides to produce **two daughter cells** that are **identical** to the original parent cell.

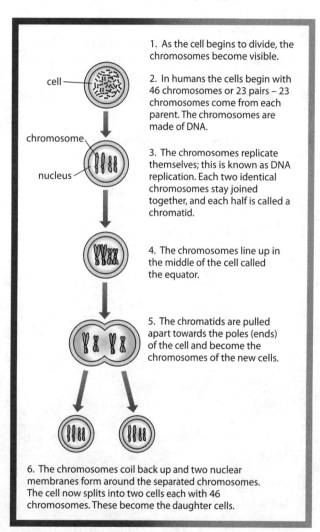

1. As the cell begins to divide, the chromosomes become visible.

2. In humans the cells begin with 46 chromosomes or 23 pairs – 23 chromosomes come from each parent. The chromosomes are made of DNA.

3. The chromosomes replicate themselves; this is known as DNA replication. Each two identical chromosomes stay joined together, and each half is called a chromatid.

4. The chromosomes line up in the middle of the cell called the equator.

5. The chromatids are pulled apart towards the poles (ends) of the cell and become the chromosomes of the new cells.

6. The chromosomes coil back up and two nuclear membranes form around the separated chromosomes. The cell now splits into two cells each with 46 chromosomes. These become the daughter cells.

DNA Replication

The chromosomes are made up of long strands of deoxyribonucleic acid (DNA for short!). **DNA has the ability to copy itself exactly.**

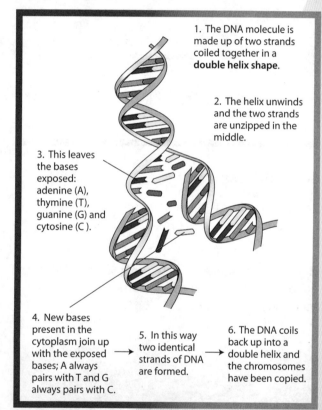

1. The DNA molecule is made up of two strands coiled together in a **double helix shape**.

2. The helix unwinds and the two strands are unzipped in the middle.

3. This leaves the bases exposed: adenine (A), thymine (T), guanine (G) and cytosine (C).

4. New bases present in the cytoplasm join up with the exposed bases; A always pairs with T and G always pairs with C.

5. In this way two identical strands of DNA are formed.

6. The DNA coils back up into a double helix and the chromosomes have been copied.

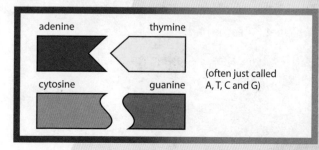

adenine   thymine

cytosine   guanine

(often just called A, T, C and G)

What Happens Next?

A zygote (fertilised egg) starts life with 46 chromosomes. It divides by mitosis to form new cells during growth. In multicellular organisms (organisms made up of more that one cell) the cells then differentiate into the different types of cell required.

Although the cells contain identical genes, they use different combinations of them according to the location in the body. Animal cells lose this ability as the animal gets older; the cells in different parts of the body can then only divide to repair and replace themselves.

Mitosis also occurs in plants during growth and replacement.

Asexual reproduction occurs through mitosis as it involves only one parent cell. It occurs in plants, for example, strawberry plants forming runners.

PROGRESS CHECK

1. How many daughter cells does mitosis produce?

2. How many chromosomes are in the daughter cells produced by mitosis in humans?

3. What are chromosomes made of?

EXAM QUESTION

1. Say whether the following statements are **true** or **false**:

    a. Mitosis produces genetically identical cells.

    b. In humans, cells produced by mitosis contain 23 chromosomes.

    c. In humans, DNA replication in mitosis makes 92 chromosomes in the nucleus.

2. Explain the significance of mitosis.

Meiosis

Meiosis is a type of cell division that occurs in the formation of gametes (sex cells). It occurs in cells in the reproductive organs (testes and ovaries in humans).

Meiosis produces cells that have half the number of chromosomes of body cells. They are called **haploid cells** and are the gametes (sex cells). In humans the haploid number is 23. Fertilisation restores the normal number of chromosomes to 46 (**diploid cells**) which are the body cells.

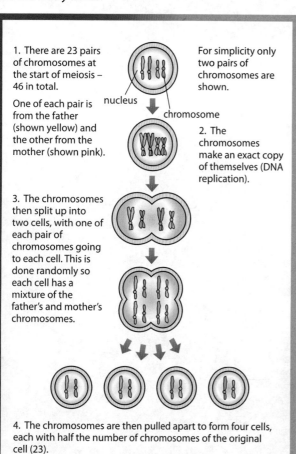

1. There are 23 pairs of chromosomes at the start of meiosis – 46 in total.

One of each pair is from the father (shown yellow) and the other from the mother (shown pink).

For simplicity only two pairs of chromosomes are shown.

nucleus

chromosome

2. The chromosomes make an exact copy of themselves (DNA replication).

3. The chromosomes then split up into two cells, with one of each pair of chromosomes going to each cell. This is done randomly so each cell has a mixture of the father's and mother's chromosomes.

4. The chromosomes are then pulled apart to form four cells, each with half the number of chromosomes of the original cell (23).

Meiosis also occurs in plants in the formation of pollen and ovules.

Sexual Reproduction and Fertilisation

In fertilisation, the male gamete joins with a female gamete to produce a fertilised egg cell called a **zygote**. During fertilisation the 23 single chromosomes in the sperm cell pair up with the 23 chromosomes in the egg cell, restoring the number of chromosomes to 46 or 23 pairs.

Meiosis and **fertilisation** give rise to **variation** in the individual, as the individual will inherit a combination of the father's and mother's genes. During meiosis it is a matter of chance which chromosomes make up the sperm and the egg, and during fertilisation it is also a matter of chance which sperm fertilises which egg. So the offspring are not genetically identical.

The environment also has an influence on an individual's characteristics. Mutations may occur during growth that would also lead to variation.

The Inheritance of Sex

When all the chromosomes are sorted into pairs, the **23rd** pair is the **sex chromosomes**. These determine whether an individual is a boy or a girl. All the other chromosomes contain information for an individual's characteristics.

A male will have one Y chromosome and one X chromosome. A female will have two X chromosomes. The female ovary will produce only X chromosome eggs during meiosis. The male testis will produce half X chromosome sperm and half Y chromosome sperm. During fertilisation, the egg may join with either an X sperm or a Y sperm.

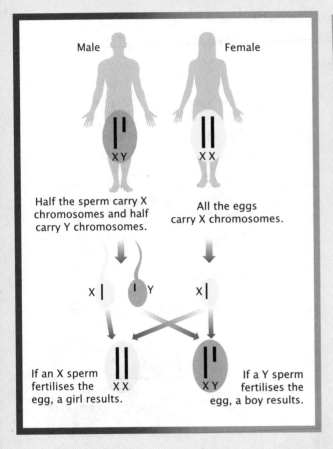

Male

Female

Half the sperm carry X chromosomes and half carry Y chromosomes.

All the eggs carry X chromosomes.

X   Y

X

If an X sperm fertilises the egg, a girl results.

X X

X Y

If a Y sperm fertilises the egg, a boy results.

PROGRESS CHECK

1. What is the scientific name for a fertilised egg?

2. How many chromosomes do human daughter cells have at the end of meiosis?

3. If the 23rd pair of chromosomes are XX will the individual be male or female?

EXAM QUESTION

1. Say whether the following statements are referring to **mitosis** or **meiosis**:

    a. Cell division that produces gametes.

    b. Produces cells that are identical.

    c. Produces cells that show variation.

2. After meiosis, how is the chromosome number restored to 46?

Genes

Inside nearly all cells is a **nucleus** that contains **instructions** controlling all our inherited characteristics. The instructions are carried on **chromosomes** that occur in pairs – one each from the mother and father.

Genes on chromosomes control particular **characteristics**. Inside human cells there are **46 chromosomes** or **23** pairs. The cell is called **a diploid cell**. Each chromosome is made up of a long-stranded molecule called **DNA**. **A gene is a section of DNA**.

Proteins and enzymes control all our characteristics. Genes are chemical instructions that code for a particular protein or enzyme and, therefore, our characteristics. Proteins are made in a process called **protein synthesis**.

There is a **pair of genes** for each feature. We call the different versions of a gene **alleles**.

Asexual reproduction involves only one parent. The offspring have exact copies of the parental genes – they are **clones**. In asexual reproduction, there is no fusing (joining) of parental gametes (sperm and eggs).

Sexual reproduction involves fertilisation and two parents. The gametes' nuclei fuse and the genes are passed on to the offspring. The offspring are not genetically identical.

DNA molecule

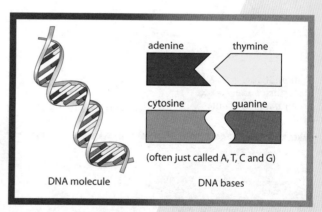

adenine   thymine

cytosine   guanine

(often just called A, T, C and G)

DNA molecule   DNA bases

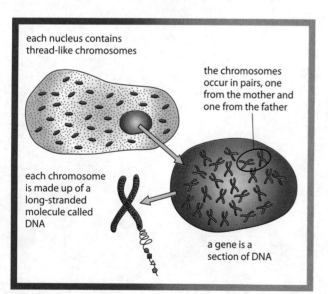

each nucleus contains thread-like chromosomes

the chromosomes occur in pairs, one from the mother and one from the father

each chromosome is made up of a long-stranded molecule called DNA

a gene is a section of DNA

A DNA molecule is joined together by chemical bases like rungs in a ladder.

There are four bases: A, T, C and G. A always pairs with T and C always pairs with G to make up the rungs of the ladder. The two sides of the ladder are coiled together to form a **double helix**.

DNA has the ability to copy itself exactly so that any new cells made have exactly the same genetic information. Each gene contains a different sequence of bases.

Inheritance

To inherit characteristics from the parent DNA, a form of reproduction needs to take place.

Protein Synthesis

Protein synthesis begins in the nucleus and ends on the ribosomes in the cytoplasm.

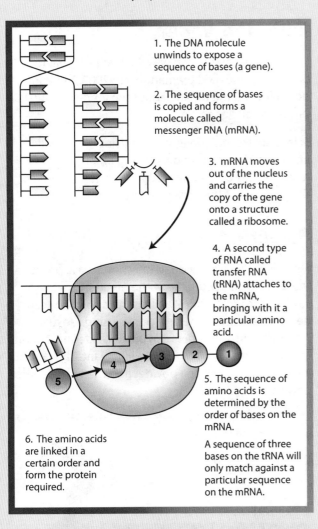

1. The DNA molecule unwinds to expose a sequence of bases (a gene).

2. The sequence of bases is copied and forms a molecule called messenger RNA (mRNA).

3. mRNA moves out of the nucleus and carries the copy of the gene onto a structure called a ribosome.

4. A second type of RNA called transfer RNA (tRNA) attaches to the mRNA, bringing with it a particular amino acid.

5. The sequence of amino acids is determined by the order of bases on the mRNA.

A sequence of three bases on the tRNA will only match against a particular sequence on the mRNA.

6. The amino acids are linked in a certain order and form the protein required.

PROGRESS CHECK

1. What are genes?

2. How many chromosomes does a human body cell have?

3. Where does protein synthesis take place?

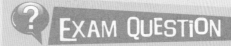

EXAM QUESTION

1. Describe the shape of a DNA molecule.

2. How are genes, chromosomes and DNA linked?

3. Explain the role DNA plays in protein synthesis.

Manipulating Life

Selective breeding is where humans try to improve animals and plants by breeding the best individuals together and hoping that it is successful. It can also be called artificial selection.

Selective Breeding in Animals

Dogs have been selectively bred over many years to produce the variety of breeds that we have today. Cows have been selectively bred to produce a greater quantity of milk. Beef cattle have been bred to produce better meat.

New techniques have been developed to produce more offspring in a shorter space of time, such as embryo transplants.

The procedure is:

- A cow is given hormones to produce many eggs.
- The eggs are fertilised.
- They are allowed to develop and then split apart to form clones.
- The embryos are then implanted into surrogate cows.

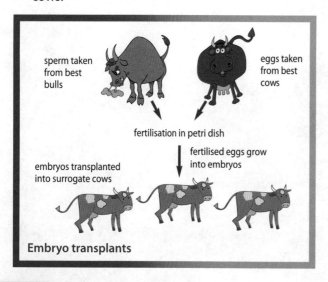

sperm taken from best bulls

eggs taken from best cows

fertilisation in petri dish

fertilised eggs grow into embryos

embryos transplanted into surrogate cows

Embryo transplants

Dolly the Sheep

In 1996, Dolly the sheep was the first mammal to be cloned. She died prematurely in 2003. Her early death fuelled the debate about the long-term health problems of clones.

Scientists are looking at ways of using genetically engineered animals to grow replacement organs for humans. This poses many ethical concerns, not least the problem of the organ being rejected.

Selective Breeding in Plants

Selectively bred individuals may not always produce the desired characteristics if the breeding involves sexual reproduction. With plants, this problem can be overcome by producing clones using asexual reproduction. Gardeners can produce identical plants by taking **cuttings** from an original plant. The cuttings are dipped in hormone powder and then grown into new plants.

From cuttings to clones
trim off lower leaves and make a slanting cut just below a leaf stalk

roots grow from stem after several weeks in water and hormone powder

Tissue culture is a technique used by commercial plant breeders. The plant breeders take just a few plant cells and grow a new plant from them using a special growth medium containing hormones. All the plants are identical to the original so the breeder can be sure of producing the desired characteristics.

Problems with Selective Breeding

If animals or plants are continually bred from the same best animals or plants then the animals and plants will all be very similar. A change in the environment may mean that the new animals or plants will not cope with the change and die out. The gene pool will then contain fewer alleles, reducing further selective breeding options.

Gene Therapy

Gene therapy is a technique for correcting defective genes responsible for disease development. In most studies, a viral vector carrying a 'normal' gene is inserted into the patient's cells to replace an 'abnormal' disease-causing gene.

At present no human gene therapy product is on the market as it is still experimental and has not proved very successful in most clinical trials. However, gene therapy as a treatment for cancer is more promising and the research continues.

There are two types of gene therapy; one focuses on treating the patient and the other on eggs and sperm, with the intention of preventing certain inherited diseases.

PROGRESS CHECK

1. What type of reproduction produces clones?

2. Are calves produced by embryo transplants, clones?

3. What is gene therapy?

? EXAM QUESTION

Mandy stated that selectively breeding plants was always successful.

a. Is this true or false? Explain your answer.

b. What techniques could be used to produce a clone of a plant?

c. Why is selective breeding in animals not always successful?

Inheritance and Disease

Genes pass on characteristics from one generation to the next. Sometimes 'faulty' genes that cause genetic diseases are inherited.

Genetics

Genetics is the study of how information is passed on through generations.

Mendel discovered the principles behind genetics by studying the inheritance of a single factor (colour) in pea plants. It wasn't until the discovery of microscopes after Mendel's death that the basic facts of cell division, sexual reproduction and consequently inheritance were understood.

Definitions

- **Gene**: the unit of inheritance carried on chromosomes. Alternative forms of a gene are called **alleles**.

- **Recessive**: only has an effect in the homozygous recessive condition.

- **Dominant**: means it is the stronger allele and has an effect in the heterozygous condition.

- **Genotype**: the type of alleles an organism carries.

- **Phenotype**: what the organism physically looks like.

- If an organism has both alleles the same they are **homozygous dominant** or **homozygous recessive**.

- If an organism has different alleles they are **heterozygous**.

A Worked Example

Letters are used to represent alleles, upper case for dominant characteristics and lower case for recessive characteristics.

The allele for brown eyes is **dominant (B)** to the **recessive** blue eyes allele (**b**).

If the mother and father are **heterozygous** for eye colour, then they have the genotype **Bb**. What colour eyes will their children have?

We can show the possible outcomes using a **genetic diagram**.

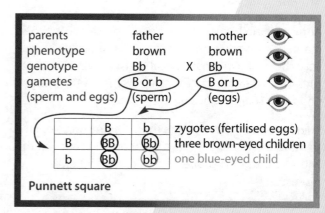

This gives a 3:1 ratio of brown to blue eyes.

Inherited Diseases

Cystic fibrosis is the commonest inherited disease in Britain. About 1 in 2000 children born in Britain has cystic fibrosis. It is caused by a **recessive allele**, c, carried by about 1 person in 20. People who have the genotype **Cc** are unaffected by the disease. They are said to be **carriers**. Only people who have the genotype **cc** are affected.

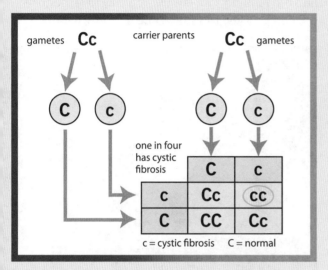

Huntington's chorea is caused by a **dominant allele (H)**. This means only one allele is needed to pass on the disease, so all **heterozygous people are sufferers (Hh)**. The only people free from the disease are **homozygous recessive (hh)**. Huntington's chorea affects 1 in 20 000 so it is a rare disease. There is a 50% chance of inheriting the disease if just one parent is heterozygous.

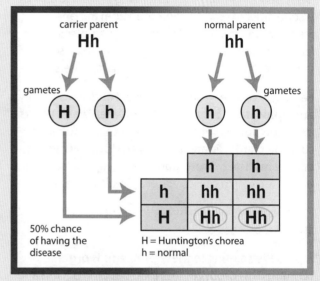

Cystic fibrosis sufferers produce large amounts of **thick, sticky mucus** that can block air passages and digestive tubes. This causes difficulty with breathing and absorbing food. The mucus **encourages bacteria to grow**, which causes chest infections. There is still no cure.

A person with the disease develops **uncontrolled jerky movements** and the **brain degenerates**. There is no cure and onset of the disease is late. The sufferer is usually about 30–40 years old before they realise that they have it. Consequently, many have already had children and passed on the disease.

PROGRESS CHECK

1. What does homozygous mean?

2. How is cystic fibrosis inherited?

3. Why are the chances of inheriting Huntingdon's chorea so high?

? EXAM QUESTION

Tongue rolling (**R**) is dominant to non-tongue rolling (**r**). David has the genotype **Rr** and Helen has the genotype **Rr**.

a. Show the possible genotypes of their children using a genetic diagram.

b. What are the possible genotypes and phenotypes for tongue rolling and non-tongue rolling?

Food Production

Farming has become more intensive to try and provide more food from a given area of land. This reduces the need to destroy the countryside for extra space for farming.

Many people regard intensive farming as cruel to animals. Also, in order to produce more food from the land, **fertilisers and pesticides** are needed. With intensive farming methods, nutrients are quickly used up so the farmer has to replace them with artificial fertilisers.

Fertilisers can be washed into rivers and lakes causing **eutrophication**. Eutrophication is when water plants grow too quickly. This causes competition for light so some plants die and are broken down by micro-organisms. The micro-organisms use up the oxygen in the water, which causes water animals to die.

Pesticides may end up in our food chains or disrupt animal food chains.

A possible solution to these problems is **organic farming**. This produces less food per area of land and can be expensive as it is labour intensive. It does, however, attempt to leave the countryside as it is and is kinder to animals.

Organic farming uses **manure** as a fertiliser, **set-aside land** to allow wild plants and animals to flourish and **biological control** of **pests**.

Intensive Farming of Animals

Farmers can restrict the movement of animals by giving them less exercise. This means the animals gain more weight and it keeps them warm. Also, the animals won't need feeding as much. Antibiotics are used to keep disease at bay. This means less labour costs which equals cheaper produce.

The disadvantages are that keeping animals confined can be classed as cruel and there is worry over the use of antibiotics – they are expensive and the fear is that they may enter the food chain.

Intensive farming examples include battery hens and fish farming. Fish farming is a way to respond to dangerously low fish stocks due to over-fishing.

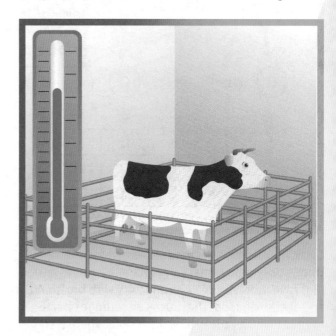

Intensive Farming of Plants

Hydroponics is the growth of plants without soil in a special medium such as peat. This is useful in areas where the soil is infertile. The plants need support and carefully controlled mineral levels. They are grown in glasshouses where factors affecting growth and diseases can be controlled. Crop yields can be improved by growing plants in ideal, climate controlled conditions like greenhouses.

The greenhouse allows the farmer or horticulturalist to control all the factors needed to **increase the rate of photosynthesis** and prevent outside influences such as birds from entering and eating the crop.

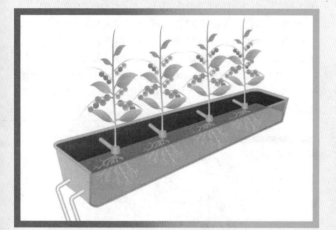

Food Distribution

Food is produced in many ways to try to meet the needs of the rising human population. Genetic modification, selective breeding and intensive farming have enabled us to produce bigger, better, faster-growing and higher-yielding plants and animals.

The problem, it seems, is not the amount of food but how it is distributed evenly around the world. Solving food distribution should be a main priority in solving world hunger.

PROGRESS CHECK

1. Why is the movement of animals restricted in intensive farming?

2. Give **one** example of intensive farming of animals.

3. Give **one** example of intensive farming of plants.

? EXAM QUESTION

Copy and complete the following table to describe **two** advantages and **two** disadvantages of organic farming and intensive farming.

	Advantages	Disadvantages
Organic Farming	1	1
	2	2
Intensive Farming	1	1
	2	2

Plant Hormones

Plant hormones are chemicals that control growth movements in plants.

Plants' respond to their surroundings to give them a better chance of survival.

Plants responses are called **tropisms** and are controlled by **hormones**. Chemical hormones control the growth of shoots and roots, flowering and the ripening of fruits. A plant's response to **light** and **gravity** is under the control of auxin.

Control of Growth

Plant growth takes place mainly in the **root tip** and **shoot tip**. These areas contain hormones called **auxins**. They move through the plant in solution by diffusion. Auxins **speed up growth in stems** and **slow down growth in roots**.

Response to Light

A plant's response to light is called **phototropism**. Plant shoots grow towards the light. Normally light shines from above. Auxin is spread evenly and the shoot grows upwards. If light comes from one side, auxin accumulates down the shaded side. The auxin makes these cells elongate and grow faster, causing unequal growth. The result is that the shoot **bends towards the light**. The shoot is **positively phototropic**.

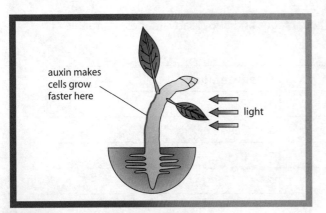

auxin makes cells grow faster here

light

Response to Gravity

A plant's response to gravity is called **geotropism**. Even if you plant a seed the wrong way up, the shoot always grows up away from gravity and the shoot grows down towards gravity. If a plant is put on its side, auxin gathers on the lower half of the shoot and root. Auxin *slows* down the growth of root cells so the root curves downwards.

auxin

auxin **slows** down the growth of root cells, while the cells on the upper half grow normally, so the root curves downwards

auxin

auxin **speeds up** the growth of shoot cells so the shoot curves upwards

Auxin *speeds up* the growth of shoot cells so the shoot curves upwards.

The roots are **positively geotropic** and the shoots are **negatively geotropic**.

Commercial Uses of Plant Hormones

Growing Cuttings

Rooting powder contains synthetic auxins. A cutting is taken from a plant and dipped in the powder. This stimulates the roots to grow quickly and enables gardeners to grow lots of exact copies of a particular plant.

Killing Weeds

Synthetic auxins are used as selective weed killers, e.g. on lawns. They only affect broad-leaved weeds – narrow-leaved grasses and cereals are not affected. Synthetic auxins kill the weeds by making them grow too fast.

Seedless Fruits

Synthetic auxins are sprayed on unpollinated flowers so the fruits form without fertilisation and without pips, e.g. seedless grapes.

Early Ripening

Plant hormones can also be used to ripen fruit in transport. Bananas and other fruits are picked when they are unripe and less easily damaged. By the time they arrive for sale, they are ripe and ready to eat.

PROGRESS CHECK

1. What is the name of the hormone that controls common plant responses?

2. Does auxin speed up or slow down growth in roots?

3. Does auxin speed up or slow down growth in shoots?

EXAM QUESTION

Bananas are often imported from other countries. They are picked when unripe but are ripened before sale.

a. Why are the bananas picked and transported when unripe?

b. How are they ripened before being sold?

c. Name another use for your answer to part b.

Plant Growth

Plants have a general basic structure and grow in a similar way to animals.

Plant Structure

A plant's basic structure is divided up into **five** parts:

1. **The flower** contains the male and female sex organs to make seeds.

2. **The stem** holds the plant **upright**. It contains hollow tubes. **Xylem** tubes carry water and **dissolved minerals** from the roots to the shoots and leaves (called **transpiration**). **Phloem** tubes are columns of living cells that carry **glucose** and other food substances made by the plant up and down the plant to growing and storage areas (called **translocation**).

3. **The root anchors** the plant in the soil and takes up **water** and **minerals** from the soil.

4. The **root hairs** absorb water and minerals from the soil by **increasing** the **surface area** of the roots for more efficient absorption.

5. **The leaf** carries out **photosynthesis**.

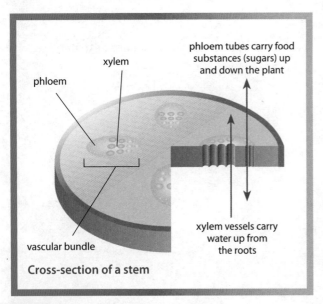

Cross-section of a stem

phloem

xylem

phloem tubes carry food substances (sugars) up and down the plant

xylem vessels carry water up from the roots

vascular bundle

Growth

Plants grow in a similar way to animals – cell division by mitosis and cell differentiation – but they also undergo a process called elongation. This is where the plant's cell vacuole absorbs water and swells. Plant cells also continue to grow, whereas animal cells eventually stop growing.

A plant's root tip and shoot tips are the only areas of a plant that are capable of cell division, so the rest of the plant grows by elongation and cell differentiation. Unlike animal cells, plant cells retain the ability to differentiate throughout life. This is demonstrated when cuttings are taken from plants. These cuttings are capable, under the right conditions, of growing into an identical plant.

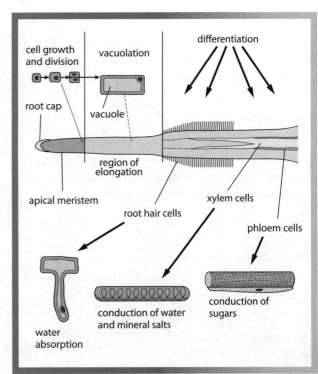

cell growth and division

vacuolation

differentiation

root cap

vacuole

region of elongation

apical meristem

xylem cells

root hair cells

phloem cells

water absorption

conduction of water and mineral salts

conduction of sugars

Factors Affecting Growth

The inheritance of genes in a plant will determine growth and shape. Environmental factors play an important part in plant growth – plants are influenced a great deal by the climate and availability of nutrients. In areas where these factors are lacking, such as the desert and in the shade, very few plants grow. In woodlands, the leaves of tall trees create a canopy that restricts light on the ground. This means the plants on the woodland floor are few and far between.

Healthy Growth

Minerals dissolved in water are absorbed from the soil by the roots. Minerals are usually present in the soil in quite low concentrations so a method called **active transport** is used to take them up into root hair cells. This requires energy and can move substances from a low concentration to a high concentration (against a concentration gradient).

Mineral	Why needed	Deficiency symptoms
Nitrates	to form proteins	stunted growth, yellow older leaves
Phosphates	role in photosynthesis and respiration, making DNA	poor root growth, purple younger leaves
Potassium	to make enzymes used in respiration and photosynthesis	yellow leaves with dead spots, poor flower and fruit growth
Magnesium	to make chlorophyll	yellow leaves

Animal Growth

Growth is an increase in size or mass of an organism.

The processes of growth in animals include cell division by **mitosis** and **differentiation** where cells become specialised for their purpose.

Each species of animal has a size range for that particular species. Human height range shows **continuous variation** – it is influenced by a number of genes, not just tall or short. There are many different heights in between the extremes.

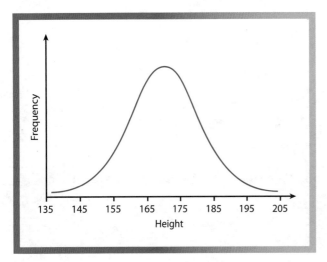

Height is also influenced by nutrition and hormones such as the growth hormone produced by the pituitary gland in the brain.

Human Growth

The main phases of human growth are: infancy, childhood, puberty, maturity and old age. Humans grow at different rates throughout these stages. In early infancy, the growth is concentrated on the trunk and head with the arms and legs getting longer at the age of six. This is because during infancy, babies are less mobile and need to concentrate on digestion (in the trunk area).

During puberty, there is a growth spurt. Then, once maturity is reached, humans actually lose a little height!

Babies in the womb have different growth rates for different parts of their body. At first the head is much larger than the rest of the body, but about half way through pregnancy, the body begins to catch up.

Once born, their weight and head size, if plotted on growth curves, can be an indication of growth problems if outside the normal ranges.

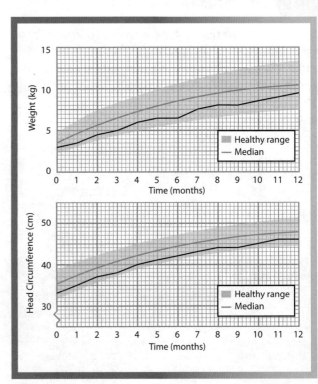

The Hayflick Limit

The Hayflick limit is named after the man who observed cells dividing in the human lungs and noticed that they only divided about 50 times and then they died. As cells approached this limit they exhibited signs of old age. This limit has been observed in all human cell types that have been fully differentiated, though it does vary from cell to cell and from organism to organism. The human limit is around 52.

Exceptions

Stem cells are cells in the body that have not yet been fully differentiated. They are found in embryos and in some adult cells such as the bone marrow. Stem cells continue to divide and regenerate throughout the organism's life.

Cancer is caused when cells grow out of control. Some tumours stop growing when they reach their limit, but some cancers find ways around the Hayflick limit and become 'immortal' malignant tumours.

Regeneration

Regeneration is the ability to re-grow parts of the body. Only certain animals can do this, and these include spiders, worms and reptiles. Lizards can re-grow their tails if they lose them in a fight. These animals have cells that are able to revert back from specialised cells to undifferentiated cells that then re-specialise.

PROGRESS CHECK

1. By what factors is human height influenced?

2. How do animals grow from a fertilised egg cell?

3. What does regeneration mean?

EXAM QUESTION

Humans grow in size and mass because their cells repeatedly divide by mitosis and then specialise.

a. What are the main phases of human growth?

b. What is the Hayflick limit?

c. Which type of cells does not have a Hayflick limit?

The Circulatory System

The circulatory system carries oxygen, food and other chemicals to all parts of the body and removes waste products.

The Heart

The circulatory system consists of the heart, blood vessels and blood. Mammals have a **double circulatory system** – the blood passes through the heart twice on one complete journey. The lower left side of the heart has much thicker walls than the right side because it pumps oxygenated blood at high pressure out of the aorta to other arteries to transport substances around the body.

The right side of the heart takes in deoxygenated blood returned from the cells and transports it to the lungs to be oxygenated.

The heart is made of **cardiac muscle**. It has its own blood supply via **coronary arteries** that supply the heart muscle with oxygen and nutrients. These arteries can become blocked and result in a heart attack. The whole heart, or parts of the heart such as valves, can be replaced. Also, if a heart beats irregularly, a pacemaker can be fitted.

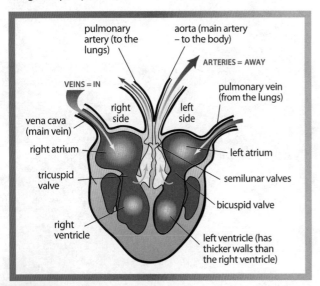

Blood

Blood is a tissue consisting of a fluid called **plasma** with **red blood cells**, **white blood cells** and **platelets** suspended in it, and various substances dissolved in it. It carries food and oxygen to the cells and removes waste products.

Red blood cells carry oxygen to all the cells of the body. They have adapted so that they can do this efficiently.

Red blood cells:

- have **no nucleus** (more room for haemoglobin)
- **are** small and **flexible** to pass through small blood vessels.

Their shape is a **small**, **biconcave disc**, which gives a maximum surface area to volume ratio for absorbing oxygen.

Red blood cells contain a substance called **haemoglobin**. In the lungs it combines with oxygen to form **oxyhaemoglobin**. In the tissues it gives up the oxygen to form haemoglobin again.

White blood cells fight disease. They have a large nucleus and are larger than red blood cells. Their shape varies.

Platelets are fragments of cells. Their function is to help with the blood clotting process. Haemophilia is a disorder whereby the blood does not clot due to a lack of platelets.

Plasma consists mainly of water, with substances such as soluble food, salts, carbon dioxide, urea, hormones, antibodies and plasma proteins dissolved in it.

Blood Vessels

Veins carry **deoxygenated** blood **back to the heart** from the body at **low pressure**. They have **valves** to prevent the blood flowing backwards. Veins have a large **lumen** (hole in the middle).

Arteries carry **oxygenated** blood **away from the heart** towards the body at **high pressure**. They have very **thick, muscular, elastic walls** to withstand the high pressure. The surge of blood through the arteries as the heart beats causes **a pulse** that can be felt in the wrist and neck.

Capillaries are only **one cell thick** and have very **thin, permeable walls** to allow oxygen and nutrients to diffuse out of them. They are the site of exchange between the blood and the cells of the body.

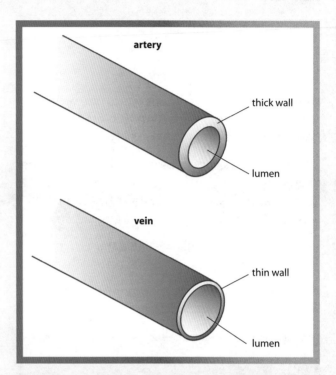

artery

thick wall

lumen

vein

thin wall

lumen

PROGRESS CHECK

1. Which blood vessels carry blood away from the heart?

2. Why do arteries have elastic, muscular walls?

3. Why do veins have valves?

EXAM QUESTION

1. Describe a red blood cell and explain how its structure makes it suitable for its function.

2. What else does blood contain?

3. How is blood transported around the body?

Atomic Structure

All atoms have the same basic structure with differing numbers of components.

Atoms

Elements are made of only one type of **atom**. An atom has a **nucleus** (which contains **protons** and **neutrons**) surrounded by shells of **electrons**.

All atoms of the same element have the same number of protons.

- Protons have a mass of 1 and a charge of 1+.
- Neutrons have a mass of 1 and no charge.
- Electrons have a negligible mass and a charge of 1−.

Atoms are neutral because they contain the same number of protons and electrons.

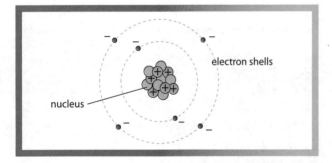

electron shells

nucleus

Bonding

Atoms can join together by:

- sharing electrons (this is called a covalent bond)
- transferring electrons (this forms ions; the attraction between oppositely charged ions is called an ionic bond).

The Periodic Table

- There are about 100 different types of element.
- These elements are often displayed in the periodic table.
- The horizontal rows are called **periods**.
- The vertical columns are called **groups**.

When the periodic table was first designed, many of the elements which we know today had yet to be discovered. Gaps were left in the table and detailed predictions were made about what the new elements would be like.

In the modern periodic table, the elements are arranged in order of increasing atomic number.

Group 1	Group 2											Group 3	Group 4	Group 5	Group 6	Group 7	Group 0
H																	He
Li	Be											B	C	N	O	F	Ne
Na	Mg											Al	Si	P	S	Cl	Ar
K	Ca	Sc	Ti	V	Cr	Mn	Fe	Co	Ni	Cu	Zn	Ga	Ge	As	Se	Br	Kr
Rb	Sr	Y	Zr	Nb	Mo	Tc	Ru	Rh	Pd	Ag	Cd	In	Sn	Sb	Te	I	Xe
Cs	Ba	La	Hf	Ta	W	Re	Os	Ir	Pt	Au	Hg	Tl	Pb	Bi	Po	At	Rn
Fr	Ra																

The modern periodic table

Mass Number and Atomic Number

Two numbers are often written next to symbols. These are the mass number and the atomic number.

The mass number tells us the number of protons added to the number of neutrons in the nucleus of one atom.

The atomic number, which is sometimes called the proton number, tells us the number of protons in the nucleus of an atom. In a neutral atom this also tells us the number of electrons.

An atom of sodium has a mass number of 23 and an atomic number of 11.

This means that this atom of sodium has:

- 11 protons (atomic number)
- 11 electrons (atomic number)
- 12 neutrons (mass number – atomic number)

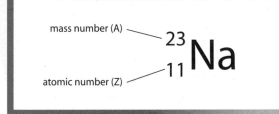

mass number (A)

atomic number (Z)

$$^{23}_{11}\text{Na}$$

Isotopes

Isotopes are different forms of the same element. This means that they have the same number of protons but a different number of neutrons.

PROGRESS CHECK

1. What is special about atoms of the same element?

2. What is the small, central part of an atom called?

3. What are found in shells around the central part of an atom?

4. How are the names and symbols of elements often displayed?

5. Roughly how many elements are there?

? EXAM QUESTION

An atom of carbon has a mass number of 13 and an atomic number of 6.

a. How many protons, electrons and neutrons does this atom of carbon have?

b. What is the mass and charge of a proton?

Electronic Structure

The electronic structure of an atom determines its characteristics and chemical nature.

Atoms

Atoms consist of a small, central **nucleus** (which contains protons and neutrons) surrounded by shells of **electrons**.

Electrons

Electrons fill up the shell closest to the nucleus (called the first shell) first. When this is full, they fill up the next shell.

In our model, there is room for up to two electrons in the first shell and up to eight electrons in the other shells.

Examples

A lithium atom has three electrons – two in the first shell and one in the second shell, giving it an electronic structure of 2,1.

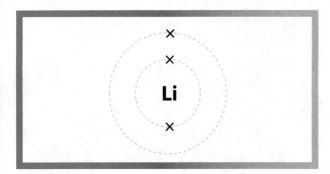

A sodium atom has eleven electrons – two in the first shell, eight in the second shell and one in the third shell, giving it an electronic structure of 2,8,1.

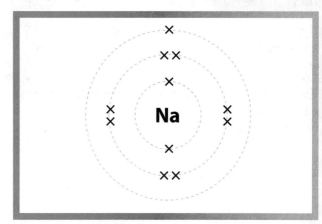

The number of electrons in the outer shell of an atom reveals the group of the periodic table that the element belongs to.

Lithium and sodium both have just one electron in their outer shell, so both belong to Group 1 of the periodic table.

A nitrogen atom has seven electrons – two in the first shell and five in the second shell, giving it an electronic structure of 2, 5.

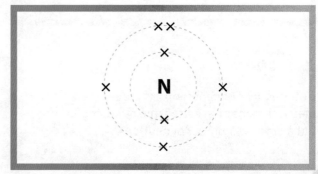

Nitrogen belongs to Group 5 of the periodic table.

A carbon atom has six electrons – two in the first shell and four in the second shell, giving it an electronic structure of 2,4.

Carbon belongs to Group 4 of the periodic table.

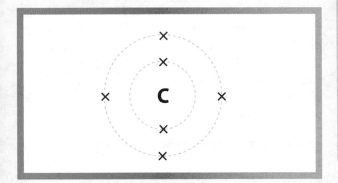

An oxygen atom has eight electrons – two in the first shell and six in the second shell, giving it an electronic structure of 2,6.

Oxygen belongs to Group 6 of the periodic table.

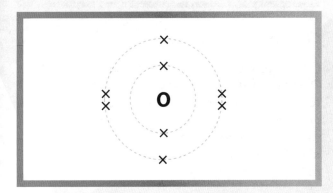

Ionic Bonding

Ionic compounds are held together by strong forces of attraction between oppositely charged ions, called ionic bonds.

Ions

An **ion** is an atom or group of atoms with a charge.

Ions have a full, outer shell of electrons (like an atom of a noble gas).

Ionic bonding involves the transfer of **electrons** between atoms to form charged ions.

Atoms that gain electrons become negatively charged, while atoms that lose electrons become positively charged.

Ionic **bonding** is the attraction between these oppositely charged ions.

Sodium Chloride

Sodium reacts with chlorine to form sodium chloride. The sodium atom transfers its outer electron to a chlorine atom. Both the sodium atom and the chlorine atom now have a full outer shell of electrons. The sodium atom that lost an electron now has a 1+ charge and is called a sodium ion, while the chlorine atom has gained an electron and now has a 1– charge and is called a chloride ion.

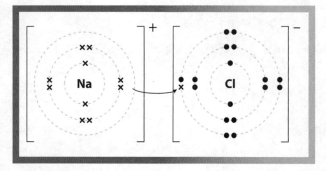

Magnesium Oxide

Magnesium reacts with oxygen to form magnesium oxide. The magnesium atom transfers its two outer electrons to an oxygen atom. The magnesium atom that lost two electrons now has a 2+ charge and is called a magnesium ion, while the oxygen atom has gained two electrons and now has a 2– charge and is called an oxide ion.

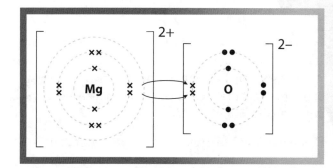

Calcium Chloride

Calcium reacts with chlorine to form calcium chloride. The calcium atom transfers its two outer electrons to two chlorine atoms. The calcium atom that lost two electrons now has a 2+ charge and is called a calcium ion, while the chlorine atoms have gained one electron each and now have a 1– charge and are called chloride ions.

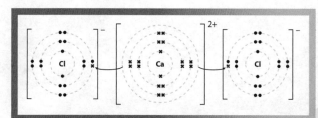

Ionic Structures

Ionic compounds have **giant structures**. They are held together by strong forces of attraction between oppositely charged ions. These forces act in all directions. This means that ionic compounds have very high melting and boiling points because lots of energy must be supplied to break these strong forces of attraction. Ionic compounds are solid at room temperature. Ionic solids do not conduct electricity because the ions are not able to move, but they do conduct when molten or when they are dissolved in something else.

Oxidation and Reduction

When sodium reacts with chlorine to form the ionic compound sodium chloride, sodium atoms lose an electron to form sodium ions.

$$Na \rightarrow Na^+ + e^-$$

This is an oxidation reaction.

Chlorine atoms gain an electron to form chloride ions.

$$Cl + e^- \rightarrow Cl^-$$

This is a reduction reaction.

PROGRESS CHECK

1. What is an ion?

2. What is the charge on an ion formed when an atom gains one electron?

3. What is the charge on an ion formed when an atom loses one electron?

4. What is the charge on an ion formed when an atom gains two electrons?

5. What is the charge on an ion formed when an atom loses two electrons?

? EXAM QUESTION

Sodium reacts with chlorine to form an ionic compound.

a. Why does this compound have a high melting point?

b. Write a word equation for the reaction.

c. Sodium atoms lose an electron to form sodium ions. What is the charge on a sodium ion?

Covalent Bonding

In covalent bonding, atoms gain a full outer shell by sharing pairs of electrons.

Covalent Bonds

A covalent bond is a shared pair of **electrons**. Non-metal atoms can gain a full, outer shell of electrons by **sharing** pairs of electrons.

Hydrogen, H_2

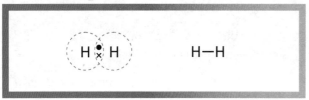

A hydrogen molecule is formed when two hydrogen atoms share a pair of electrons. Both atoms now have a full, outer shell of electrons.

Hydrogen Chloride, HCl

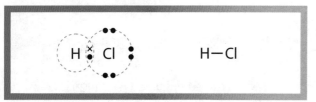

A hydrogen chloride molecule is formed when a hydrogen atom and a chlorine atom share a pair of electrons. Both atoms now have a full, outer shell of electrons.

Methane, CH_4

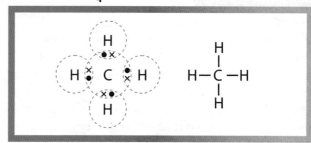

A methane molecule consists of a carbon atom surrounded by four hydrogen atoms. The carbon atom shares a pair of electrons with each of the hydrogen atoms.

Ammonia, NH_3

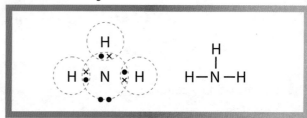

An ammonia molecule consists of a nitrogen atom surrounded by three hydrogen atoms. The nitrogen atom shares a pair of electrons with each of the hydrogen atoms.

Water, H_2O

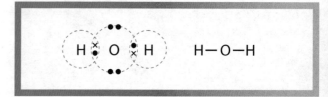

A water molecule consists of an oxygen atom and two hydrogen atoms. The oxygen atom shares a pair of electrons with each of the hydrogen atoms.

Oxygen, O_2

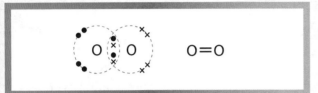

An oxygen molecule consists of two oxygen atoms. The atoms share two pairs of electrons. So they are joined by a double covalent bond.

Types of Structures

There are two types of covalent structure:

◼ simple covalent structures

◼ giant covalent structures.

Simple Covalent Structures (Simple Molecules)

Simple covalent structures are formed by small numbers of atoms. There are very strong forces of attraction within these molecules, but much weaker forces of attraction between one molecule and another. This means that simple covalent structures have low melting and boiling points and most are liquids or gases at room temperature. They do not conduct electricity because they do not contain ions or free electrons.

Giant Covalent Structures (Macromolecular)

Giant covalent structures include:

◼ diamond

◼ graphite

◼ silicon dioxide.

They consist of very large numbers of atoms. All the atoms are held together by strong covalent bonds, so they have high melting and boiling points and are solid at room temperature.

They do not conduct electricity (except graphite) because they do not contain ions and they do not have free electrons. They are insoluble in water.

PROGRESS CHECK

1. Give the formula of a hydrogen molecule.

2. Give the formula of a hydrogen chloride molecule.

3. Give the formula of a methane molecule.

4. Give the formula of an ammonia molecule.

5. Give the formula of an oxygen molecule.

EXAM QUESTION

A water molecule consists of an oxygen atom covalently bonded to two hydrogen atoms.

a. What is a covalent bond?

b. What is the formula of water?

c. Why does water have quite a low melting point?

Alkali Metals

The alkali metals belong to **Group 1** of the periodic table. All have similar properties as they have one electron in their outer shell.

The alkali metals include:

- lithium
- sodium
- potassium.

They are found on the far left-hand side of the periodic table.

Group 1 metals have similar properties because they have similar electron structures. Alkali metals react with non-metals to form ionic compounds. The alkali metal atom loses an electron to form an ion with a 1+ charge.

$$Na \rightarrow Na^+ + e^-$$

The alkali metal atom is oxidised.

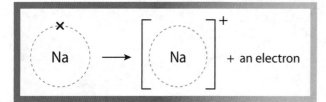

If sodium metal is burnt in chlorine gas the compound sodium chloride is formed.

$$sodium + chlorine \rightarrow sodium\ chloride$$

The reaction can also be summed up as:

$$2Na_{(s)} + Cl_{2(g)} \rightarrow 2NaCl_{(s)}$$

(s) indicates that the substance is a solid.
(g) indicates that the substance is a gas.

There are two other state symbols:

(l) indicates that the substance is a liquid.
(aq) indicates that the substance is aqueous or dissolved in water.

Group 1 metals form white compounds that dissolve in water to form colourless solutions.

All the alkali metals are very **reactive**. They react vigorously with water to form a metal hydroxide and hydrogen. For this reason they are stored under oil.

Lithium, sodium and potassium are all less dense than water. This means that if a small piece of metal is placed onto a trough of water the metal floats on top of the water as it reacts.

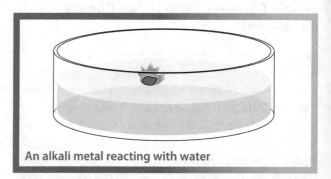

An alkali metal reacting with water

Example

lithium	+ water	→ lithium hydroxide	+ hydrogen
2Li	$+ 2H_2O \rightarrow$	2LiOH	$+ H_2$
sodium	+ water	→ sodium hydroxide	+ hydrogen
2Na	$+ 2H_2O \rightarrow$	2NaOH	$+ H_2$
potassium	+ water	→potassium hydroxide	+ hydrogen
2K	$+ 2H_2O \rightarrow$	2KOH	$+ H_2$

Lithium is the least reactive of these three metals. Potassium is the most reactive.

There is a gradual increase in reactivity down the group. This is because the outer electron is further from the nucleus so it is lost more easily.

Flame Tests

Flame tests can be used to identify the metals in compounds. The colour of the flame indicates the **metal** present:

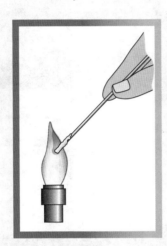

■ lithium – red

■ sodium – orange

■ potassium – lilac.

PROGRESS CHECK

1. Where are the alkali metals found in the periodic table?

2. Which of these metals would react most vigorously with water: sodium, lithium or potassium?

3. Name the gas produced when an alkali metal reacts with water.

4. What colour is seen when a flame test is carried out on a sodium compound?

5. What colour is seen when a flame test is carried out on a potassium compound?

EXAM QUESTION

Sodium reacts with water to form sodium hydroxide and hydrogen.

a. Write a word equation for this reaction.

b. Write a balanced symbol equation for this reaction.

c. Why must sodium be stored under oil?

d. When potassium reacts with water the reaction is more vigorous than when sodium reacts with water. Why does potassium react more vigorously?

Noble Gases and Halogens

The noble gases and halogens are found on the right of the periodic table. They have various uses according to their properties.

The horizontal rows in the **periodic table** are called periods. The vertical columns are called groups. Elements in the same group have the same number of electrons in their outer shell, so they have similar chemical properties.

The Noble Gases

The noble gases include:

- helium
- neon
- argon.

They are found on the far right-hand side of the periodic table. All the noble gases are very **unreactive** because they have a full, stable outer shell of electrons. This can make them very useful.

- Helium is **less dense** than air, so if a balloon is filled with helium gas it will float. Helium balloons are popular decorations at parties and special events.

- Neon is widely used in electrical discharge tubes.

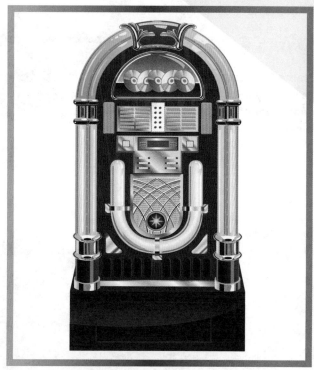

- Argon is used to make filament lamps.

The Halogens

The halogens include:

- fluorine
- chlorine
- bromine
- iodine.

They are found next to the noble gases in the periodic table.

Chlorine is a pale green gas, bromine is a brown liquid and iodine is a dark grey solid. This shows us that the **boiling point** of the halogens increases as you go down the group.

Chlorine is used to sterilise water and in the manufacture of pesticides and plastics. Iodine is used to sterilise cuts.

The halogens react vigorously with alkali metals to form metal **halides**. The reaction between sodium and chlorine can be summed up by the equation:

$$\text{sodium} + \text{chlorine} \rightarrow \text{sodium chloride}$$

$$2Na \ + \ Cl_2 \ \rightarrow \ 2NaCl$$

The halogen atom, chlorine, gains an electron to form a chloride ion, Cl^-. This is a **reduction** reaction.

Sodium chloride is used in food preparation as a flavouring (common salt) and as a preservative. It is also used in the production of chlorine gas.

There is a gradual decrease in reactivity as you go down the group, so chlorine is more reactive than bromine and iodine. This is because when an atom reacts to form an ion, the electron is placed into a shell increasingly further away from the nucleus.

A more reactive halogen will displace a less reactive halogen from its solution. So chlorine will **displace** bromine from a solution of potassium bromide.

chlorine + potassium bromide → potassium chloride + bromine

$$Cl_2 \ + \ 2KBr \ \rightarrow \ 2KCl \ + \ Br_2$$

PROGRESS CHECK

1. Which group does iodine belong to?

2. Which group does neon belong to?

3. In what state is bromine at room temperature?

4. What is helium used for?

5. What is argon used for?

? EXAM QUESTION

Chlorine and bromine both belong to the same group of the periodic table.

a. What group do they belong to?

b. Chlorine is more reactive than iodine. Write a word equation to sum up the reaction between chlorine and potassium iodide.

Calculations

Calculations of relative atomic mass and relative formula mass are useful for estimating the amount of product formed in a reaction.

Relative Atomic Mass

Relative atomic mass is used to compare the mass of different atoms. The relative atomic mass of an element is the weighted average mass of the isotopes of the element compared with an atom of carbon-12 which has a mass of 12.

Relative Formula Mass

Relative formula mass is worked out by adding together the relative atomic masses of the atoms in the ratio indicated by the chemical formula.

Example

Water, H_2O

Relative atomic mass of hydrogen = 1

Relative atomic mass of oxygen = 16

The relative formula mass of water
$$= (1 \times 2) + (16 \times 1)$$
$$= 18$$

Moles

The relative formula mass of a substance in grams is known as one mole of the substance, so one mole of water has a mass of 18 g.

Calculating the Mass of a Product

We can work out the theoretical yield of a reaction from a balanced symbol equation.

Example

Hydrogen reacts with oxygen to form water.

$$2H_2 + O_2 \rightarrow 2H_2O$$

If 4 g of hydrogen is burnt, what is the theoretical yield of water produced?

The relative formula mass of $H_2 = 2$

The relative formula mass of $H_2O = 18$

The number of moles of 4 g of $H_2 = \dfrac{4g}{2g}$
$$= 2 \text{ moles.}$$

From the balanced symbol equation:

2 moles of hydrogen makes 2 moles of water.

The mass of 2 moles of water $= 2 \times 18 = 36\,g$

Percentage Yield

The amount of product made in a reaction is called the yield. We often find that the actual yield of a reaction is lower than the theoretical yield.

This could be for a number of reasons, including:

- The reaction is reversible and does not go to completion.

- Some of the product was lost, for example during filtering or evaporation.

- There may be side reactions that are producing another product.

The percentage yield of a reaction =

$$\frac{\text{actual amount of product}}{\text{theoretical yield}} \times 100\%$$

Example

The theoretical yield for a reaction is calculated as 1.2 g.

A student carries out the reaction but only produces 1.0 g of product.

The percentage yield $= \frac{1.0}{1.2} \times 100\% = 83.3\%$

Atom Economy

The atom economy of a reaction =

$$\frac{\text{mass of useful product}}{\text{total mass of product}} \times 100\%$$

Scientists try to choose reactions that have a high atom economy.

PROGRESS CHECK

1. What is relative atomic mass used for?

2. What is the standard against which we measure the relative atomic mass of different atoms?

3. What is one mole equal to?

4. Why might a reversible reaction have a low percentage yield?

5. What is the equation for the percentage yield of a reaction?

EXAM QUESTION

A student calculates that the theoretical yield for her experiment is 2.5 g. She carries out the experiment and only produces 2.2 g of product.

a. Why might her actual yield be less than her theoretical yield?

b. What is the percentage yield of this reaction?

Haber Process

Ammonia is a very useful raw material in the manufacture of fertilisers and cleaning fluids.

Making Ammonia

The Haber process is used to make ammonia, NH_3. Nitrogen (from the fractional distillation of liquid air) is reacted with hydrogen (from natural gas) in a reversible reaction.

The reaction can be summed up as:

$$\text{nitrogen} + \text{hydrogen} \rightleftharpoons \text{ammonia}$$

$$N_{2(g)} + 3H_{2(g)} \rightleftharpoons 2NH_{3(g)}$$

The state symbol (g) means gaseous – a gas.

The forward reaction is exothermic.

On cooling, the ammonia liquefies and can be removed. Any unreacted nitrogen and hydrogen are recycled. The ammonia is produced all the time in a continuous process. Ammonia is used in the manufacture of fertilisers and cleaning fluids.

In a closed system, eventually an equilibrium is reached. The relative amount of the substances at equilibrium depends on the conditions.

The conditions chosen in the Haber process are typically:

- an iron catalyst

- a high pressure of around 200 atmospheres

- a moderate temperature of around 450 °C.

An iron catalyst increases the rate of reaction. Catalysts are often used in industry because they allow us to use less energy.

A high pressure is used to increase the yield of ammonia. Increasing the pressure favours the forward reaction which has fewer gas molecules on the product side.

The forward reaction is exothermic so a high temperature would give a good rate of reaction but a poor yield of ammonia. A low temperature would give a poor rate of reaction but a good yield of ammonia. In practice, a compromise temperature is used which gives a reasonable rate and a reasonable yield.

Fertilisers

Fertilisers help crops to grow bigger and faster. They replace the essential elements including nitrogen, phosphorus and potassium used by plants as they grow. Plants absorb these elements through their roots.

Many fertilisers can be made by a neutralisation reaction between an acid and an alkali.

Ammonia can be oxidised and then reacted with water to form nitric acid. This can be reacted with ammonia to form the popular fertiliser ammonium nitrate.

$$\text{nitric acid} + \text{ammonia} \rightarrow \text{ammonium nitrate}$$

$$HNO_3 + NH_3 \rightarrow NH_4NO_3$$

In a similar way, reacting ammonia with sulfuric acid forms ammonium sulfate, while reacting ammonia with phosphoric acid forms ammonium phosphate.

Percentage by Mass

Plants use nitrogen to produce protein. Being able to calculate the percentage of nitrogen in a fertiliser allows us to choose the right amount of fertiliser to use.

Percentage mass of an element in a compound =

$$\frac{\text{relative atomic mass of the element} \times \text{number of atoms}}{\text{relative formula mass of the compound}} \times 100\%$$

The percentage of nitrogen in ammonium nitrate, NH_4NO_3

$$= \frac{14 \times 2}{80} \times 100\%$$

$$= 35\%$$

So the percentage of nitrogen in ammonium nitrate is 35%.

PROGRESS CHECK

1. Where is nitrogen obtained from?

2. Where is hydrogen obtained from?

3. What is the catalyst used in the Haber process?

4. What is the temperature used in the Haber process?

5. What is the pressure used in the Haber process?

? EXAM QUESTION

Many plant fertilisers contain nitrogen.

a. What do plants use nitrogen for?

b. What is ammonia reacted with to make the fertiliser ammonium nitrate?

c. Calculate the percentage by mass of nitrogen in ammonia.

Rates of Reaction

The rate of reaction tells us how fast a chemical reaction takes place. A chemical reaction takes place when reacting particles **collide** and have enough **energy** to react – this is called the activation energy.

Increasing the Rate of Reaction

Temperature

When the **temperature** is increased:

- particles move faster
- they collide more often
- when they do collide, they have more energy so more have enough energy to react
- so the rate of reaction increases.

Concentration

When the **concentration** of a solution is increased:

- the particles collide more often
- so the rate of reaction increases.

Concentrations are measured in moles per cubic decimetre, $mol\ dm^{-3}$.

Pressure

When the **pressure** of gases is increased:

- the particles collide more often
- so the rate of reaction increases.

Surface Area

When the **surface area** of a solid is increased (small pieces have a big surface area):

- the particles collide more often
- so the rate of reaction increases.

Catalyst

Adding a **catalyst** increases the rate of a chemical reaction. Catalysts are specific to certain reactions. They are not used up during reactions so they can be reused many times. Catalysts are used in industry to reduce production costs. Enzymes are biological catalysts.

Following a Reaction

When magnesium metal is reacted with dilute hydrochloric acid, a salt called magnesium chloride and the gas hydrogen are made.

> magnesium + hydrochloric acid → magnesium chloride + hydrogen

We can follow how fast this reaction happens by measuring:

- how quickly the hydrogen gas is made
- how quickly the mass of the reaction flask goes down as the hydrogen gas is made and escapes from the flask.

This graph shows the amount of hydrogen produced in two experiments.

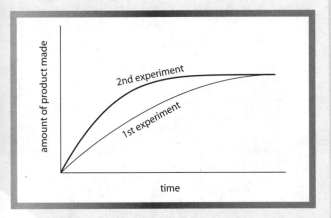

In both experiments the rate of reaction is fastest at the start of the reaction.

The reaction is over when the line levels out.

The second experiment has a faster rate of reaction than the first experiment.

PROGRESS CHECK

1. What needs to happen for two particles to react?

2. How does increasing temperature affect the rate of a chemical reaction?

3. How does decreasing the concentration of a solution affect the rate of a chemical reaction?

4. How does adding a catalyst affect the rate of reaction?

5. During an experiment when is the rate of reaction fastest?

? EXAM QUESTION

Copy and complete the sentences using the words below:

increases   catalysts   decreases   reactants

_____ a. _____ increase the rate of a reaction but they are not used up themselves so they can be used many times. In the reaction between magnesium and hydrochloric acid increasing the surface area of the magnesium _____ b. _____ the rate of reaction. Decreasing the concentration of the hydrochloric acid _____ c. _____ the rate of reaction.

The reaction is over when one of the _____ d. _____ is used up.

Energy

In all chemical reactions, energy is either given out or taken in.

Exothermic Reactions

In **exothermic** reactions energy (normally in the form of heat) is transferred to the surroundings. This means that if we recorded the temperature change during the reaction, we would see a temperature increase.

Most reactions are exothermic.

The fuel used in Bunsen burners is called methane. When methane is burnt it reacts with oxygen to release heat energy.

Neutralisation reactions are also exothermic. If sodium hydroxide solution is reacted with hydrochloric acid heat energy is released.

The burning of fuels, rusting and neutralisation are all examples of exothermic reactions.

Rusting is an exothermic reaction

Endothermic Reactions

In **endothermic** reactions, energy (normally in the form of heat) is taken in from the surroundings. This means that if we recorded the temperature change during the reaction we would see a temperature decrease.

Thermal decomposition reactions are endothermic.

Bonds

- Energy must be supplied to break **bonds**.

- Energy is released when new bonds are made.

- In exothermic reactions, more energy is released when new bonds are formed than is taken in to break old bonds.

- In endothermic reactions, more energy is taken in to break the old bonds than is released when the new bonds are formed.

Burning is an exothermic reaction

The table below shows some average bond energies.

Bond	Bond energy kJ mol^{-1}
C—C	347
O=O	498
C—H	413
O—H	464
C—O	358
H—Cl	432

Some reactions are **reversible**. They can go in a forward or in a reverse direction. If A and B are reactants and C and D are products, then a reversible reaction can be summed up by:

$$A+B \rightleftharpoons C+D$$

If the forward reaction is exothermic, the reverse reaction is endothermic and the same amount of energy is transferred in each case.

When blue, hydrated copper sulfate is heated it decomposes to form white, anhydrous copper sulfate and water. This reaction is endothermic.

If water is added to anhydrous copper sulfate it forms hydrated copper sulfate. This reaction is exothermic and can be used to test that a liquid is really water.

The reactions can be summed up by the equation:

hydrated copper sulfate $\rightleftharpoons$ anhydrous copper sulfate + water

Ammonia is an important chemical that is used to make fertilisers. Hydrogen reacts with nitrogen to produce ammonia. The reaction is reversible and can be summed up by the equation:

hydrogen + nitrogen $\rightleftharpoons$ ammonia
$$3H_2 + N_2 \rightleftharpoons 2NH_3$$

PROGRESS CHECK

1. Is the burning of a fuel an exothermic or endothermic reaction?

2. If there is a temperature decrease during a chemical reaction, what type of reaction has taken place?

3. What is released when a new bond is made?

4. What does the symbol $\leftrightarrow$ indicate?

5. What type of reaction is thermal decomposition?

? EXAM QUESTION

When hydrated copper sulfate is heated it forms anhydrous copper sulfate and water. The reaction is reversible.

a. Write a word equation for this reaction.

b. What would you **see** when hydrated copper sulfate was heated?

c. How could you prove that a colourless liquid was really water?

Aluminium

Aluminium is extracted from its ore by electrolysis and has many uses.

Pure aluminium has a low **density** but is too soft for many uses. Aluminium can be mixed with other metals to form **alloys**. These alloys combine low density with high strength.

Extraction

Aluminium is quite a reactive metal. It is extracted from its ore, **bauxite**, by **electrolysis**. This is an expensive process because it involves lots of steps and requires lots of energy.

Bauxite contains aluminium oxide. For electrolysis to occur, the aluminium ions and the oxide ions must be able to move. So solid aluminium oxide must be heated until it melts or dissolves in something else.

Aluminium oxide has a very high melting point, so heating aluminium oxide until it melts would be very expensive. Fortunately, another aluminium ore called **cryolite** has a much lower melting point. In practice, aluminium oxide is dissolved in molten cryolite.

During electrolysis the Al^{3+} ions move to the negative electrode (cathode) where aluminium forms.

$$Al^{3+} + 3e^- \rightarrow Al$$

The aluminium ions are **reduced**.

The oxide ions, O^{2-} move to the positive electrode (anode) where they react to form oxygen molecules.

$$2O^{2-} \rightarrow O_2 + 4e^-$$

The oxide ions are **oxidised**.

The oxygen reacts with the **graphite** anode to produce carbon dioxide so these electrodes must be regularly replaced.

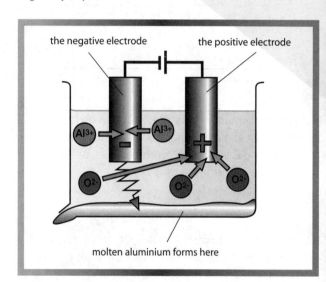

the negative electrode   the positive electrode

Al^{3+} Al^{3+}

O^{2-} O^{2-} O^{2-}

molten aluminium forms here

The Electrolysis of Dilute Sulfuric Acid

The electrolysis of dilute sulfuric acid produces **oxygen** and **hydrogen**.

Hydrogen is formed at the cathode.

$$2H^+ + 2e^- \rightarrow H_2$$

Oxygen is formed at the anode.

$$4OH^- \rightarrow 2H_2O + O_2 + 4e^-$$

Gas Tests

Hydrogen	Oxygen
Burns with a 'squeaky' pop	Relights a glowing splint

Uses of Aluminium

Aluminium appears to be much less reactive than it really is. This is because aluminium objects quickly react with oxygen to form a layer of aluminium oxide, which prevents any further reaction from occurring.

Uses of aluminium include:

- drinks cans
- bicycles
- aeroplanes.

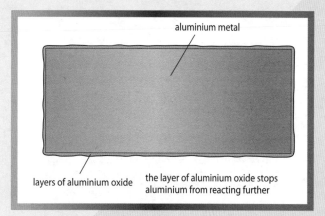

aluminium metal

layers of aluminium oxide

the layer of aluminium oxide stops aluminium from reacting further

PROGRESS CHECK

1. What is the chemical compound found in bauxite?

2. Bauxite is one ore of aluminium. Name another ore of aluminium.

3. Does solid aluminium oxide conduct electricity?

4. Does molten aluminium oxide conduct electricity?

5. In the electrolysis of aluminium oxide what is formed at the negative electrode?

? EXAM QUESTION

Aluminium is extracted from aluminium oxide by electrolysis.

a. During electrolysis aluminium is deposited at the negative electrode. Give the symbol equation for this reaction.

b. Oxygen is produced at the positive electrode. Give the symbol equation for this reaction.

c. Why must the graphite electrodes be regularly replaced?

Sodium Chloride

Sodium chloride is a type of salt. Salts are very important compounds with many uses.

Uses of salts include:

- the production of fertilisers
- as colouring agents
- in fireworks.

Sodium Chloride Solution

Sodium chloride (common salt) is a very important resource. It is found in large quantities dissolved in seawater and in underground deposits formed when ancient seas evaporated.

Rock salt (unpurified salt) is used in winter to grit roads to stop them from becoming icy and dangerous.

The **electrolysis** of concentrated sodium chloride solution produces:

- chlorine
- hydrogen
- sodium hydroxide.

During electrolysis, positive hydrogen H+ ions move to the negative electrode (cathode) where hydrogen is produced.

$$2H^+ + 2e^- \rightarrow H_2$$

Chloride ions, Cl^-, move to the positive electrode (anode) where chlorine is produced.

$$2Cl^- \rightarrow Cl_2 + 2e^-$$

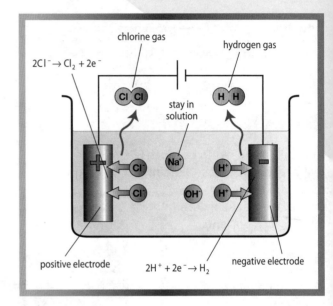

Gas tests:

- Hydrogen burns with a 'squeaky' pop.
- Chlorine bleaches damp litmus paper.

Uses:

- Chorine is used to sterilise water.
- Hydrogen is used in the manufacture of margarine.
- Sodium hydroxide is also produced and is used in the production of soaps.

Solid Sodium Chloride

Solid sodium chloride does not conduct electricity because the ions cannot move. If sodium chloride is heated until it melts, then electrolysis can occur.

The electrolysis of molten sodium chloride produces chlorine and sodium.

Chloride ions, Cl^- move to the positive electrode (anode) where chlorine is produced.

$$2Cl^- \rightarrow Cl_2 + 2e^-$$

Positive sodium, Na^+ ions move to the negative electrode (cathode) where sodium is produced.

$$Na^+ + e^- \rightarrow Na$$

Copper

Copper is a very useful metal. It is:

- a good electrical conductor
- a good thermal conductor
- very unreactive.

Copper is widely used for electrical wiring and plumbing. Traditionally, we extract copper from its ores and then purify it using electrolysis.

Insoluble Salts

Some salts are **insoluble**. They can be made by reacting solutions of soluble salts.

Here, insoluble barium sulfate is made by reacting a solution of barium chloride with a solution of sodium sulfate. The reaction also produces sodium chloride.

The barium sulfate is a precipitate.

barium chloride	+	sodium sulfate	→	barium sulfate	+	sodium chloride
$BaCl_{2\,(aq)}$	+	$Na_2SO_{4\,(aq)}$	→	$BaSO_{4\,(s)}$	+	$2NaCl_{(aq)}$

The state symbol (aq) means aqueous (it is dissolved in water).

The state symbol (s) means it is solid.

PROGRESS CHECK

1. Give **one** use of salts.

2. Name an insoluble salt.

3. Give the word equation for the reaction between barium chloride and sodium sulfate.

4. What does the state symbol (s) indicate?

5. What does the state symbol (aq) indicate?

EXAM QUESTION

Sodium chloride is an important resource.

a. The electrolysis of concentrated sodium chloride solution produces two gases. Chlorine is produced at the positive electrode. Which gas is produced at the negative electrode?

b. Give the equation for the reaction at the positive electrode that produces chlorine.

c. Give **one** use of chlorine.

Making Salts

Salts are very important compounds. They can be made by reacting acids with metals, metal carbonates, metal oxides or metal hydroxides.

- Hydrochloric acid forms **chloride** salts.

- Nitric acid forms **nitrate** salts.

- Sulfuric acid forms **sulfate** salts.

Sulfuric acid is used in the manufacture of fertilisers and in car batteries.

Solutions

If a solution has a pH of 7 it is **neutral**. If the pH is less than 7 it is an **acid** and if the pH is more than 7 it is an **alkali**.

Strong acids like nitric acid, sulfuric acid and hydrochloric acid have a low pH, typically 1 or 2.

Acids react with bases to form a salt and water.

The reaction between an acid and a base is called **neutralisation**.

An alkali is a soluble base.

Acidic solutions contain **hydrogen**, H^+ ions. Alkaline solutions contain **hydroxide**, OH^- ions.

During **neutralisation** reactions, hydrogen ions react with hydroxide ions to form water, which is neutral.

$$H^+_{(aq)} + OH^-_{(aq)} \rightarrow H_2O_{(l)}$$

The state symbol (l) means it is a liquid.

Metals

Fairly reactive metals react with acids to form a salt and hydrogen.

magnesium +	hydrochloric acid	→	magnesium chloride	+ hydrogen
Mg +	2HCl	→	$MgCl_2$	+ H_2

Metal Carbonates

Metal carbonates react with acids to form a salt, water and carbon dioxide.

calcium carbonate	+	hydrochloric acid	→	calcium chloride	+ water +	carbon dioxide
$CaCO_3$	+	2HCl	→	$CaCl_2$	+ H_2O +	CO_2

The metal carbonate is added to the acid until the reaction stops (there is no more fizzing). The excess metal carbonate is then filtered off leaving a salt solution. If the salt solution is warmed carefully the water evaporates leaving crystals of the salt.

The more gently the salt solution is warmed and the longer the time taken for the crystals to form, the larger they will be.

Metal Oxides

Metal oxides react with acids to form a salt and water.

copper oxide + nitric acid → copper nitrate + water

$$CuO \quad + \quad 2HNO_3 \quad \rightarrow \quad Cu(NO_3)_2 \quad + \quad H_2O$$

Metal Hydroxides

Metal hydroxides also react with acids to form a salt and water.

potassium hydroxide + nitric acid → potassium nitrate + water

$$KOH \quad + \quad HNO_3 \quad \rightarrow \quad KNO_3 \quad + \quad H_2O$$

An indicator can be used to show when the acid and alkali have completely reacted.

Ammonia

Ammonia reacts with water to form a weak alkali. Ammonia can be reacted with acids to form ammonium salts.

ammonia + hydrochloric acid → ammonium chloride

$$NH_3 \quad + \quad HCl \quad \rightarrow \quad NH_4Cl$$

PROGRESS CHECK

1. If a solution has a pH of 7 what type of solution is it?

2. If a solution has a pH of 10 what type of solution is it?

3. If a solution has a pH of 2 what type of solution is it?

4. Name the salt made when magnesium reacts with hydrochloric acid.

5. Name the salt made when calcium carbonate reacts with hydrochloric acid.

EXAM QUESTION

Egg shells contain calcium carbonate. If hydrochloric acid is placed on an egg shell the acid reacts with the calcium carbonate.

a. Write a word equation to sum up this reaction.

b. Suggest a value for the pH of hydrochloric acid.

Metals

Metals all have similar properties because of their atomic structure. Metals have many uses.

Metallic Bonding

The atoms in a pure metal have a regular arrangement. This means that the atoms can slide over each other quite easily so metals can be bent into shape, or drawn into wires.

Metals can be mixed to form alloys. In alloys the atoms have different sizes so it is harder for the layers of atoms to pass over each other. This makes alloys harder than pure metals.

In metals, the **electrons** in the outermost shell of an atom are **delocalised** and free to move throughout the whole structure. This means that metals consist of positive metal ions and negative delocalised electrons.

Metallic bonding is the attraction between these positive metal ions and the negative delocalised electrons. This is an **electrostatic** attraction.

Metals are good thermal and electrical conductors because the delocalised electrons are free to move throughout the structure.

Metals have high melting points because of the strong forces of attraction between the metal ions and the delocalised electrons.

Metal Carbonates

When metal **carbonates** are heated, they decompose to form a metal oxide and carbon dioxide. This is known as a thermal decomposition reaction. If carbon dioxide is bubbled through limewater it turns the limewater cloudy.

copper carbonate → copper oxide + carbon dioxide
$$CuCO_3 \rightarrow CuO + CO_2$$

iron carbonate → iron oxide + carbon dioxide
$$FeCO_3 \rightarrow FeO + CO_2$$

manganese carbonate → manganese oxide + carbon dioxide
$$MnCO_3 \rightarrow MnO + CO_2$$

zinc carbonate → zinc oxide + carbon dioxide
$$ZnCO_3 \rightarrow ZnO + CO_2$$

We can tell that a chemical reaction has taken place when there is a change of colour which shows us that a new substance has been formed.

Hydroxide Tests

We can identify the metals present in metal salt solutions by adding sodium **hydroxide solution**.

If the metal ion forms a **precipitate** we can use the colour of the precipitate to identify the metal present:

■ copper(II) – pale blue precipitate

■ iron(II) – green precipitate

■ iron(III) – brown precipitate.

Transition Metals

Transition metals are found in the middle of the periodic table.

Many transition metals and their compounds are useful catalysts.

Iron is used in the manufacture of ammonia and nickel is used in the manufacture of margarine.

Most iron is made into the alloy **steel** which is used to make cars and bridges because it is strong and cheap.

Copper is used to make **brass** which is used in electrical wiring because it is a good electrical conductor.

Superconductors

Some metals behave as **superconductors** at very low temperatures.

Superconductors are special because when they conduct electricity, they have very little or no resistance. Use of superconductors will be limited until we can develop types that will work at room temperature.

PROGRESS CHECK

1. What is metallic bonding?

2. What are mixtures of metals called?

3. What is the catalyst used in the manufacture of ammonia?

4. What is the catalyst used in the manufacture of margarine?

5. What is the test for carbon dioxide?

? EXAM QUESTION

Transition metals are strong and hard.

a. Name an alloy of iron used to make cars.

b. Name an alloy of copper used in electrical wiring.

Water

Water is a very important resource that needs to be conserved.

Water can be used as:

- a coolant
- a raw material to make new chemicals from
- a solvent.

Water Pollution

Water can be polluted by:

- nitrates from fertiliser runoff
- lead compounds from lead pipes
- pesticides sprayed near to water resources.

Nitrate Problems

Fertilisers are used to help plants to grow better, but they can enter waterways and cause problems.

The nitrates in fertilisers can cause algae to grow at a fast rate. Eventually the algae die and bacteria begin to decompose them. The bacteria use up the oxygen in the water. Fish and other aquatic life cannot get enough oxygen and may die. This is called eutrophication.

In the UK, water is taken from areas that are well away from any sources of pollution, including:

- lakes
- rivers
- aquifers (rocks that contain water)
- reservoirs.

There is only a limited supply of fresh water, so it is important that we conserve water when we can.

Water Purification

In developing nations clean, safe water is extremely important.

In the water purification process:

- any large pieces of debris such as sticks are removed
- the water is filtered to remove suspended particles such as clay
- the water is passed through filter beds of charcoal and sand to remove unpleasant smells and make the water taste better
- finally, the water is chlorinated to reduce the number of micro-organisms to acceptable levels.

Water is only taken from safe sources

Seawater

Water can be obtained from seawater by distillation but this takes a lot of energy and is only used where fuel is very cheaply available.

Insoluble Salts

Some salts are **insoluble**. They can be made by reacting solutions of soluble salts.

We can use a solution of silver nitrate to test for chloride, bromide or iodide ions.

- If silver nitrate is added to a solution that contains chloride ions, we see a white precipitate of silver chloride.

- If it is added to a solution that contains bromide ions, we see a cream precipitate of silver bromide.

- If it is added to a solution that contains iodide ions, we see a pale yellow precipitate of silver iodide.

PROGRESS CHECK

1. What is an aquifer?

2. During purification, why is water filtered?

3. Why is water chlorinated?

4. Why is distillation not widely used to purify water?

5. What compounds found in fertilisers can cause environmental problems?

EXAM QUESTION

We can test for the presence of chloride ions in a solution by adding silver nitrate solution.

a. What would you see if the solution contained chloride ions?

b. What is the name of the silver compound that forms?

c. What is the state of the silver compound?

Detergents

Detergents dissolve fat and grease. They are widely used as cleaning agents.

Washing Powders

We use washing powders to help get our clothes clean. They have lots of ingredients, including:

- **detergents** to remove the dirt from the fabric
- water softeners to remove the hardness from the water
- bleaches to remove stains
- **enzymes** that help to remove stains at low temperatures; this helps consumers to save money and helps to protect the environment
- optical brighteners to make the clothes look really clean.

Washing-up Liquids

We use washing-up liquids to help us to clean crockery. They have lots of ingredients, including:

- a detergent to get the crockery clean
- water to dilute the detergent so it is easier to use

- fragrance and colouring to make the washing-up liquid more attractive
- water softener to make hard water softer
- a rinsing agent that helps the water to drain away from the crockery.

Water is a good **solvent** for most ionic compounds. If a compound **dissolves**, we say it is **soluble** and the mixture that is made is called a solution.

Grease and fats do not dissolve well in water. We can use detergents to remove them from surfaces.

Many detergents are salts made by a neutralisation reaction between an acid and an alkali.

Detergent molecules have two parts: a **hydrophilic** head group that is attracted to water molecules and a **hydrophobic** part that avoids water but is attracted to fat or grease. The detergent molecules surround the fat or grease stain, which can then be washed off.

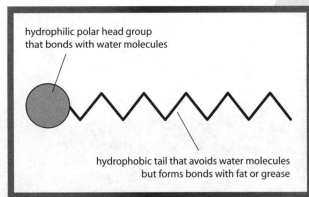

hydrophilic polar head group that bonds with water molecules

hydrophobic tail that avoids water molecules but forms bonds with fat or grease

Washing Symbols

Washing symbols on clothes show the conditions that should be used to clean the garment.

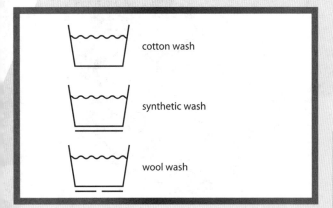

The temperature shown on the label is the maximum temperature that should be used. A lower temperature could be used but may not get the clothes as clean.

Dry Cleaning

Some fabrics can be damaged by washing them in water or may be stained with something that does not dissolve in water. These clothes can be dry cleaned. In dry cleaning, the clothes are washed in a solvent other than water. This solvent is then extracted and the clothes are carefully pressed.

PROGRESS CHECK

1. Why are bleaches added to washing powders?

2. Why are enzymes used in some washing powders?

3. Why are colouring and fragrance added to washing-up liquids?

4. Why is a rinsing agent added to washing-up liquids?

5. On a washing symbol, what does the number indicate?

? EXAM QUESTION

Detergents are an important ingredient in washing powders.

a. Why are detergents used?

b. Many detergents are salts. What should be added to an alkali to make a salt?

c. Name the end of the detergent molecule that is attracted to water molecules.

Special Materials

Some materials have special properties that make them unique and extremely useful.

Smart Materials

Smart materials are very special materials which have one or more **property** that can be dramatically changed by changes in the environment.

Thermochromic pigments can be added to paints. If these paints are heated, the colour of the paint changes. Applications include designs on cups that appear when hot liquids are added.

Nitinol is another smart material. When a force is applied, nitinol stretches but when it is warmed up, it returns to its original shape.

Nano Particles

Nanoparticles consist of just a few hundred atoms, so they are incredibly small. Present uses of these materials include sunscreens. Future uses could include better, smaller computers.

Forms of Carbon

Diamond, graphite and fullerene are all **allotropes** (forms) of the element carbon.

Buckminsterfullerene, C_{60}

Fullerenes consist of cages of carbon atoms held together by strong covalent bonds. These cages can be used to hold other molecules. Scientists are developing ways of delivering drugs using fullerenes. The most stable fullerene is called buckminsterfullerene. It has the formula C_{60}.

Buckminsterfullerene is a black solid that dissolves in petrol to form a deep red solution.

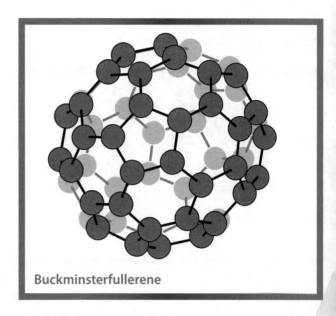

Buckminsterfullerene

Nanotubes

Fullerenes can be made into **nanoubes**. Nanotubes are very hard and strong. They can be made into lightweight sports equipment like tennis racquets. Other uses of nanotubes include industrial catalysts and semi-conductors for use in electrical circuits.

Diamond

Diamond is a highly valued gemstone. High-quality diamonds are **lustrous** and colourless and are used in jewellery. Diamonds can also be used to make cutting tools.

Diamond has a giant covalent structure. Each carbon atom is bonded to four other carbon atoms by strong covalent bonds. Diamond has a very high melting point and is hard because it has lots of bonds. It does not conduct electricity because there are no free electrons or ions to move.

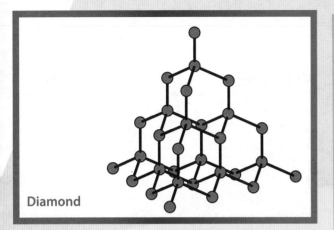
Diamond

Graphite

Graphite is used in pencil leads, as a lubricant and to make electrodes. In graphite, each carbon atom is bonded to three other carbon atoms in the same layer by strong covalent bonds.

Graphite has a high melting point because it has lots of strong covalent bonds. There are much weaker forces of attraction between the layers. This means that the layers of carbon atoms can pass easily over each other.

Graphite conducts electricity because the electrons in the weaker bonds between layers are able to move.

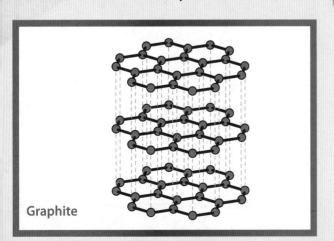
Graphite

PROGRESS CHECK

1. Give **one** use of graphite.

2. What is the formula of buckminsterfullerene?

3. Name **three** allotropes of carbon.

4. Why are diamonds used in jewellery?

5. What colour is solid buckminsterfullerene?

EXAM QUESTION

Diamonds have a very high melting point and do not conduct electricity.

a. Describe the structure of diamond.

b. Why does diamond have a high melting point?

c. Why does diamond not conduct electricity?

Vegetable Oils

Vegetable oils are important foods. They are a good source of **energy** and of vitamins A and D.

Vegetable oils can also be used as **biofuels**. When they are burnt they release lots of energy. Today we depend on fossil fuels like crude oil, but as supplies of these run out, biofuels will become increasingly important.

Popular vegetable oils include sunflower oil and olive oil. Vegetable oils can be produced from seeds, nuts and fruits. First the plant material is crushed, then the oil is extracted.

Vegetable oils can be extracted from the fruits, seeds and nuts of some plants

Vegetable oils are unsaturated because they contain carbon double bonds. We can check this by adding bromine water. The bromine water changes colour from brown to colourless. If a fat contains one double bond, it is **monounsaturated**.

Some vegetable oils contain many carbon double bonds. These are described as **polyunsaturated** fats. Doctors believe that polyunsaturated fats are better for our health than monounsaturated fats.

Animal Fats

Animal fats are usually solid at room temperature. They are saturated fats because they have no carbon double bonds. Vegetable oils are usually liquid at room temperature. They are unsaturated fats because they have carbon double bonds. These bonds affect the way that the molecules can pack together.

Unsaturated fat molecules cannot pack as closely as saturated fat molecules so unsaturated fats have lower melting points.

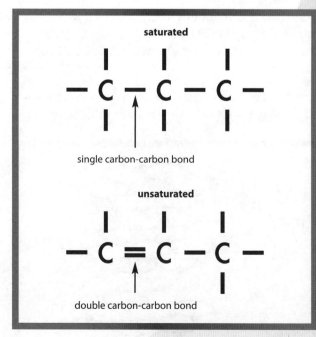

Hydrogenated Vegetable Oils

Most vegetable oils are liquids at room temperature. Liquid oils can be very useful, but there are times when we might prefer a solid fat, for example, when we want to spread it onto bread or use it to make cakes.

Vegetable oils can be made solid at room temperature by a process known as hydrogenation. The vegetable oils are heated with hydrogen using a **nickel catalyst** at around 60 °C.

PROGRESS CHECK

1. What vitamins are found in vegetable oils?

2. Name **two** types of vegetable oil.

3. Which parts of plants can we extract vegetable oils from?

4. Why can vegetable oils be described as 'unsaturated'?

5. How many double bonds does a monounsaturated fat have?

EXAM QUESTION

Copy and complete the table using the words below:

monosaturated   **bromine water**   **biofuel**   **polyunsaturated**

Name	Description
a.	a fat with one carbon double bond
b.	a fat with many carbon double bonds
c.	a material made from living organisms that can be burnt to release energy
d.	a chemical used to test for a carbon double bond

Alkanes and Alkenes

Alkanes and alkenes are hydrocarbons consisting of carbon and hydrogen atoms only. Carbon atoms form four bonds with other atoms while hydrogen atoms only form one bond.

Cracking

Fractional distillation of crude oil produces large amounts of long hydrocarbon molecules. These long molecules can be broken down into smaller, more useful and more valuable molecules by **cracking**. In this process, large molecules are heated until they evaporate and then passed over a catalyst.

Here decane is cracked to produce octane and ethene.

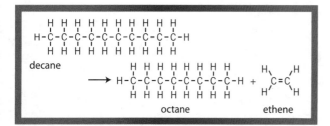

No. carbon atoms in hydrogen chain	Temperature	Fraction collected
3	less than 40°C	refinery gas
8	40°C	petrol
10	110°C	naphtha
15	180°C	kerosene
20	250°C	diesel
35	340°C	oil
50+	above 340°C	bitumen

Cracking is an example of a thermal decomposition reaction

Alkanes

The **alkanes** are a family of **hydrocarbon** molecules. Alkanes are saturated hydrocarbons because they do not contain carbon double bonds. Short alkane molecules are useful fuels.

Alkanes have the general formula C_nH_{2n+2}.

The lines in these structural diagrams represent covalent bonds.

Name	methane	ethane	propane	butane
Chemical formula	CH_4	C_2H_6	C_3H_8	C_4H_{10}
Structure	H–C–H	H–C–C–H	H–C–C–C–H	H–C–C–C–C–H

Alkenes

The **alkenes** are another family of hydrocarbon molecules. Alkenes are produced during cracking.

Alkenes are unsaturated hydrocarbons because they do contain carbon double bonds. Alkene molecules are more reactive than alkane molecules.

They can be used to make new chemicals including plastics.

Alkenes have the general formula C_nH_{2n}.

Name	ethene	propene
Chemical formula	C_2H_4	C_3H_6
Structure	$\begin{array}{c} H \quad\quad H \\ C=C \\ H \quad\quad H \end{array}$	$\begin{array}{c} H \quad\quad H \\ C=C-C-H \\ H \quad H \quad H \end{array}$

Industrial Alcohol

Ethanol can also be made from non-renewable sources. Ethanol produced in this way is called industrial alcohol.

Ethene, which is produced by the cracking of long-chain hydrocarbons, is reacted with steam to produce ethanol.

> ethene + steam → ethanol
>
> $C_2H_4 + H_2O \rightarrow C_2H_5OH$

PROGRESS CHECK

1. What is the general formula of an alkane?

2. Give **one** use for a short alkane molecule.

3. What do the lines in structural diagrams represent?

4. How can alkenes be made?

5. What is the general formula of an alkene?

? EXAM QUESTION

Ethanol can be made by reacting ethene with steam.

a. What family does ethene belong to?

b. Ethene is 'unsaturated'. What does this mean?

c. Write a word equation for the reaction of ethene with steam.

Polymers

Polymers are large molecules made of long chains of smaller molecules called monomers.

Polymerisation

In **addition polymerisation**, many small molecules are joined together to form a bigger molecule. The small molecules are called **monomers**. These monomers are unsaturated molecules. The bigger molecule is called a polymer. Plastics are **polymers**.

$$n \quad \begin{array}{c} H \quad H \\ | \quad | \\ C=C \\ | \quad | \\ H \quad H \end{array} \rightarrow \left(\begin{array}{c} H \quad H \\ | \quad | \\ C-C \\ | \quad | \\ H \quad H \end{array} \right)_n$$

The formation of polythene from ethene monomers

$$n \quad \begin{array}{c} CH_3 \quad H \\ | \quad | \\ C=C \\ | \quad | \\ H \quad H \end{array} \rightarrow \left(\begin{array}{c} CH_3 \quad H \\ | \quad | \\ C-C \\ | \quad | \\ H \quad H \end{array} \right)_n$$

The formation of polypropene from propene monomers

Properties of Plastics

The structure and bonding within a material affects its properties.

The stronger the forces between the particles in a solid, the higher the temperature at which the solid melts.

Modifying the structure of a polymer can influence its properties:

- Adding a **plasticiser** can make a plastic more flexible.

- Lengthening the polymer chain increases the forces of attraction between the molecules and increases the melting point of the polymer.

- Making the polymer chains more aligned increases the forces of attraction between the molecules and increases the melting point.

- Some plastics consist of long polymer chains with very little cross linking between the chains. When these plastics are heated the chains untangle and the plastic softens. This means that these plastics can be reshaped many times.

- Other plastics consist of polymer chains that are heavily **cross linked**. These polymers must be shaped when they are first made. When they are heated again they will not soften but may eventually burn.

Problems with Plastics

Plastics are very useful, but most plastics are **non-biodegradable**. This means that when plastic objects are thrown away, they remain in the environment and this can cause problems, including:

- landfill sites filling up more quickly

- production of toxic gases when plastics are disposed of by burning them

- recycling plastics because there are many different types and it is hard to separate them out.

To reduce these problems, scientist have developed a range of plastics that are biodegradable.

Uses of Plastics

Polythene is a very popular plastic. It is cheap and strong and is widely used to make plastic bags and bottles.

Poly vinyl chloride or **PVC** is another popular plastic. It is rigid, weatherproof and can be used to make fences and drain pipes. If it is mixed with a plasticiser it becomes more flexible and can be used to make wellington boots and macintoshes.

Polypropene is very strong and has a high elasticity. It is widely used to make crates and ropes.

Polystyrene is cheap, has a low density and can be moulded into different shapes. It is widely used in packaging.

PROGRESS CHECK

1. Name the polymer made from propene.

2. How does adding a plasticiser affect a plastic?

3. What happens when a heavily cross-linked polymer is heated?

4. Why can burning some plastics cause problems?

5. Why is it difficult to recycle plastics?

EXAM QUESTION

Polythene is a polymer.

a. Name the monomer used to make polythene.

b. Which hydrocarbon family does the monomer used to make polythene come from?

c. What is the general formula of this hydrocarbon family?

Motion

The motion of a moving object can be described using measurements of distance, time, speed, velocity and acceleration.

Speed

Speed is a measure of how fast something is going, usually measured in m/s. For example, an object that covers a distance of 3 m every second has a speed of 3 m/s.

$$\text{speed} = \frac{\text{distance}}{\text{time}}$$

- ◼ Increasing the speed **increases** the distance covered in the **same** time.

- ◼ Increasing the speed **reduces** the amount of time needed to cover the **same** distance.

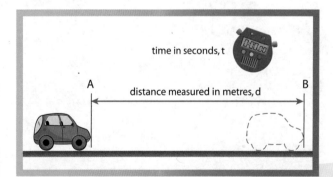

time in seconds, t

A

distance measured in metres, d

B

If the car travels a distance AB of 20.0 m in a time t = 5.0 s, its average speed is:

$$\frac{20.0\,\text{m}}{5.0\,\text{s}} = 4.0\,\text{m/s}$$

Speed cameras generally take two photographs a certain time apart and near marked lines on a road. This is because they need to measure the distance travelled in a certain time.

Velocity

Velocity is a measure of how fast something is going in a given direction. Its units are also m/s. The difference between speed and velocity is that velocity includes the direction whereas speed does not.

$$\text{average velocity} = \frac{\text{displacement}}{\text{time}}$$

Speed has magnitude (size) only – it is a **scalar** quantity.

Velocity has magnitude and direction – it is a **vector** quantity.

Acceleration

Acceleration is a measure of how fast the velocity is changing. The velocity could be increasing or decreasing.

- ◼ If velocity is constant, the change in velocity is zero and the acceleration is 0 m/s per second or 0 m/s/s.

- ◼ If velocity increases by 1 m/s every second, the acceleration is 1 m/s/s.

- ◼ If velocity increases by 2 m/s every second, the acceleration is 2 m/s/s.

- ◼ If velocity decreases by 2 m/s every second, the acceleration is –2 m/s/s; this is often called deceleration.

Acceleration is calculated using the following equation.

$$\text{acceleration} = \frac{\text{change in velocity}}{\text{time taken}}$$

$$\text{or} \quad a = \frac{(v - u)}{t}$$

where v = final velocity and u = initial velocity

The unit of acceleration, m/s/s is sometimes written as: m/s^2.

To measure acceleration, the velocity must be measured at two different times. This can be done with light gates.

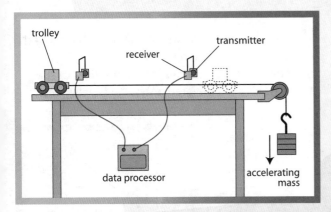

The data processor measures the velocity at two different points and measures the time between them. It calculates the acceleration using the equation: $a = \frac{(v - u)}{t}$.

Sometimes, only the **direction** of a moving body changes. For example, a planet may rotate around the Sun at a constant speed. In this case:

- Speed is constant.

- Velocity is changing because the direction is changing.

- The planet is accelerating because the velocity is changing.

PROGRESS CHECK

1. Why do speed cameras generally take two photographs a certain time apart and near marked lines on a road?

2. What is the equation that relates average velocity, displacement and time?

3. Find the average velocity of a car that travels 300 m in 15 s.

4. Explain the difference between speed and velocity.

5. When a car turns a corner at constant speed, is there a change in velocity?

EXAM QUESTION

1. State the equation for acceleration.

2. What is the acceleration of a car that accelerates from 10 m/s to 30 m/s in 4.0 s?

3. Find the deceleration of the car if it slows from 30 m/s to 0 m/s in 3.0 s.

4. If a data processor is used to measure the acceleration of a vehicle, what **three** pieces of information does it need?

Graphs for Motion

Motion graphs show how far something has travelled, how fast it is travelling and how fast it has been travelling along its journey.

Distance–Time Graphs

Distance–time graphs measure distance from a certain point. For example, the distance a car is from a tree.

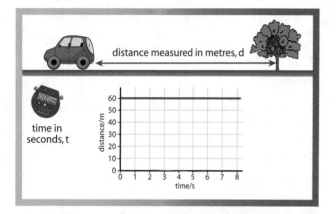

The car is stationary, 60 m away from the tree. There is no change in distance from the tree.

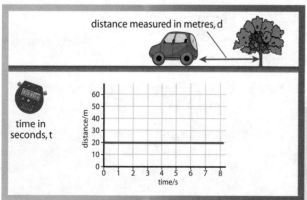

The car is stationary again, this time 20 m away from the tree.

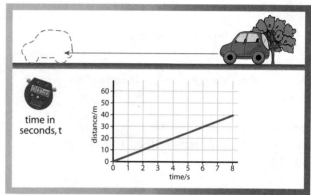

Here, the car is moving. After 4.0 s the car has moved 20 m. After 8.0 s the car has moved 40 m.
The speed of the car is equal to the gradient of the graph. In this case the gradient is $\frac{40\,m}{8.0\,s}$ = 5.0 m/s.

This graph has a steeper gradient, so the speed is greater.

The speed is $\frac{60\,m}{6.0\,s}$ = 10 m/s

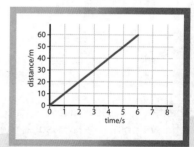

This graph has an increasing gradient which indicates an increasing speed. The car is accelerating.

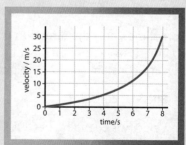

Velocity-Time Graphs

A velocity–time graph shows how the speed or velocity of an object changes with time.

- The **gradient** is equal to the **acceleration**.
- The **area** under the graph is equal to the **distance travelled**.

The velocity–time graph on the right is for a car. It shows a steady speed of 5.0 m/s.

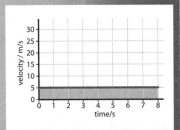

- The gradient is zero so the acceleration is 0 m/s/s.
- The area under the graph is 5.0 m/s × 8.0 s = 40 m. The car has travelled a distance of 40 m.

This graph shows more complicated motion.

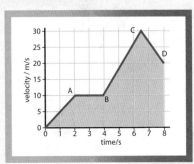

From the origin to A:

- the acceleration = $\dfrac{10\,\text{m/s}}{2.0\,\text{s}} = 5.0\,\text{m}$
- the distance travelled = $\dfrac{(10\,\text{m/s} \times 2.0\,\text{s})}{2}$
  $= 10\,\text{m}$

From B to C:

- the acceleration is $\dfrac{20\,\text{m/s}}{2.5\,\text{s}} = 8\,\text{m/s/s}$
- the distance is
  $(10\,\text{m} \times 2.5\,\text{s}) + (\dfrac{20\,\text{m/s} \times 2.5\,\text{s}}{2}) = 50\,\text{m}$

From C to D the gradient is negative, so the acceleration is negative. The car is slowing down.

PROGRESS CHECK

1. What does the gradient represent on a distance–time graph?

2. What would a steeper line represent on a distance–time graph?

3. What does the gradient represent on a velocity–time graph?

4. How can you find the distance from a velocity–time graph?

5. What does a negative gradient represent on a velocity–time graph?

? EXAM QUESTION

The graph below shows a skydiver falling through the sky.

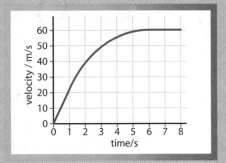

Show on the graph the following points:
a. minimum velocity
b. maximum velocity
c. minimum acceleration
d. maximum acceleration.

When Forces Combine

Forces are vector quantities. They have both magnitude and direction.

Free Body Diagrams

This **free body diagram** shows the forces acting on a girl standing on a plank. There are other forces acting on the plank and on the ground, but the free body diagram only considers the forces that act on a single body (in this case, the girl).

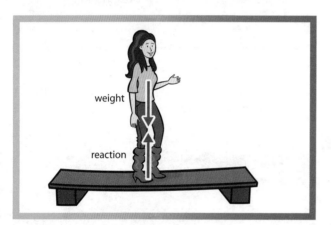

The girl experiences the force of gravity acting down and the reaction force of the plank acting up. These forces are the same size, so they cancel out. There is no net force and the girl stays still. The girl is in equilibrium.

The picture below shows a free body diagram for a plane at constant velocity.

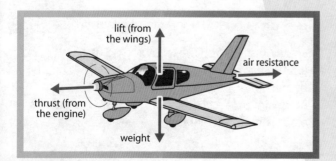

The upward and downward forces on the plane cancel out. The forwards and backwards forces also cancel out. Because the plane is already moving, this means that the plane continues to move at the **same velocity**. The plane is also in equilibrium.

The picture below shows a free body diagram for a parachutist.

The parachutist experiences weight and air resistance. Since these forces are not equal at the point illustrated, there is a net resultant force downwards.

If weight equals 400 N and the air resistance equals 80 N, the net or resultant force is 320 N in a downward direction. The parachutist is accelerating downwards; he is not in equilibrium.

Note that these two forces are in opposite directions. Therefore, the resultant force is found by subtraction. If the forces are in the same direction, the resultant force is found by adding.

Action and Reaction

Whenever two bodies interact, the forces they exert on each other are equal and opposite. An action force produces an equal and opposite reaction force. These forces are always:

- equal in magnitude
- opposite in direction
- the same type of force
- on **different** bodies.

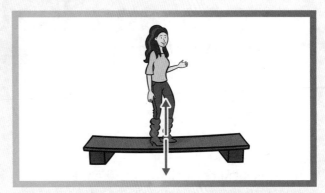

The plank experiences the contact force of the girl and it pushes back with an upward contact force of the same magnitude. Compare the forces in this diagram with the free body diagram of the girl on page 88.

page 88

PROGRESS CHECK

1. What is a free body diagram?
2. Sketch a free body diagram for a parachutist accelerating.
3. If the weight in your diagram is equal to 550 N and the air resistance is equal to 150 N, what is the resultant force on the parachutist?
4. Consider the man below. Why does the boat move backwards as he steps forwards?
5. Identify the action and the reaction forces for the man and the boat.

EXAM QUESTION

Consider the diagram below.

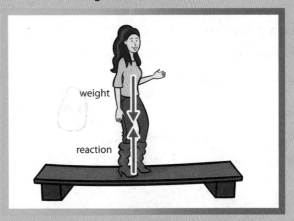

weight

reaction

a. The two forces acting on the girl are equal and opposite. Are they an example of an action and a reaction?
b. Give a reason for your answer.
c. What is the action force that causes the reaction force of the bench upwards on the girl?
d. What is the name given to the above diagram?

Forces and Motion

A force can cause an object to move; it can also cause a moving object to stop moving or change its speed or its direction.

Resultant Force

If the resultant force on a body is zero, it will remain stationary or continue to move at the same speed in the same direction.

If the resultant force on a body is not zero, it will accelerate in the direction of the resultant force.

Acceleration is always caused by a resultant force.

The force can be calculated as follows:

$$\text{force} = \text{mass} \times \text{acceleration} \qquad F = ma$$

For a given mass:

- ■ more force = more acceleration
- ■ less force = less acceleration

For a given force:

- ■ more mass = less acceleration
- ■ less mass = more acceleration

Terminal Velocity

A falling skydiver experiences a force called weight (gravity) towards the centre of the Earth.

$$\text{weight} = \text{mass} \times \text{gravitational field strength (g)}$$

On Earth, g is about 10 N/kg.

Initially, weight is the only force. As the skydiver falls drag, or air resistance begins to work against the motion.

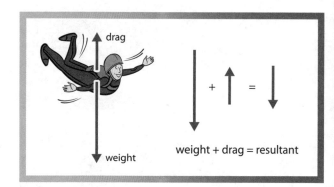

weight + drag = resultant

These two forces combine to produce a resultant force in a downward direction. The sky diver accelerates.

The acceleration produces increased velocity. This produces more drag.

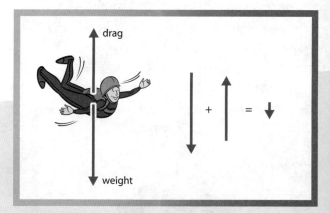

The resultant force is less so the acceleration is less.

The acceleration continues to increase velocity and hence drag. Eventually drag becomes equal in magnitude to weight.

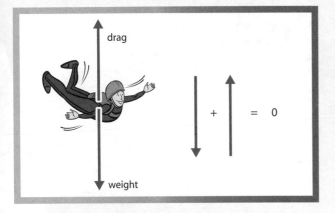

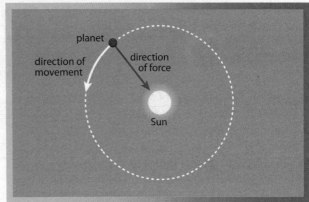

Now the skydiver has reached **terminal velocity**, the maximum velocity attainable. The skydiver continues to fall with constant velocity; there is no further acceleration. The forces are balanced, the skydiver is in equilibrium.

An object with greater surface area, or a less **streamlined** shape has greater drag. For example, a parachutist experiences greater air resistance for the same velocity. He therefore reaches terminal velocity sooner. Terminal velocity will be lower than for the skydiver.

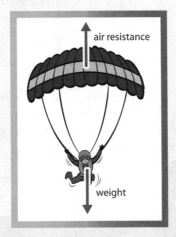

When there is no atmosphere, such as in space, there is no air resistance.

Forces for Circular Motion

An object moving in a circle is accelerating due to its direction changing.

The resultant force that causes this acceleration acts towards the centre of the circle. For a mass on a string, this force is provided by the tension in the string. For an orbiting planet, this force is provided by the gravitational pull on the planet.

PROGRESS CHECK

1. A 20 N force is applied to an object of 2.0 kg. What is the acceleration?

2. How would a top box on a car affect air resistance?

3. Does a skydiver or a parachutist experience greater air resistance?

4. Why does a parachutist have lower terminal velocity than a skydiver of the same weight?

5. What is the direction of the force needed for circular motion?

EXAM QUESTION

a. Sketch a diagram of a parachutist accelerating through the air.

b. Label air resistance and weight in your diagram.

c. Under what circumstances does the skydiver stop accelerating?

d. What is the velocity known as at this point?

Momentum and Stopping

The force required to stop a moving object depends on the object's momentum.

Momentum

When calculating what happens to bodies as a result of explosions or collisions, it is often more useful to think in terms of momentum than energy.

A faster-moving body has more kinetic energy; it also has more **momentum**.

> momentum (kgm/s) = mass (kg) × velocity (m/s)

A car of mass 1000 kg travelling at 6 m/s has momentum of 6000 kgm/s.

Momentum has **magnitude** and **direction**.

- When a force acts on a body that is moving, or able to move, a change in momentum occurs.

- Momentum is conserved in any collision/explosion providing no external forces act on the bodies.

Consider a trolley of 1.0 kg travelling at 3.0 m/s colliding with a stationary trolley of mass 2.0 kg.

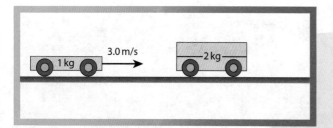

If, after the collision, the first trolley stops and the second trolley begins to move, the velocity of the second trolley can be found.

> momentum before = momentum afterwards
>
> (1.0 kg × 3.0 m/s) + (2.0 kg × 0 m/s) =
> (1.0 kg × 0 m/s) + (2.0 kg × speed after)
>
> Speed of second trolley after collision = 1.5 m/s.

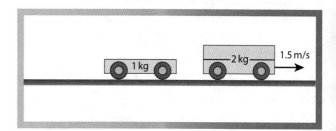

Momentum is conserved when a rocket is propelled through space. The momentum of fuel ejected in a certain time is equal to the change in momentum of the rocket during that time.

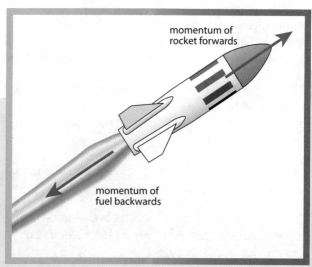

momentum of rocket forwards

momentum of fuel backwards

Stopping

- A vehicle at greater speed requires more braking force to stop in a certain distance.

- A vehicle of greater mass requires more braking force to stop in a certain distance.

The force needed to stop a car is found by considering the change in momentum:

$$\text{change in momentum} = \text{force} \times \text{time}$$

For a car of mass 1200 kg travelling at 20 m/s stopping, the momentum change is:

$$1200 \text{ kg} \times 20 \text{ m/s} = 24\,000 \text{ kgm/s}.$$

To stop in 6.0 s the brakes must exert a force of:

$$\frac{24\,000 \text{ kgm/s}}{6.0 \text{ s}} = 4000 \text{ N}.$$

If the braking time is reduced to 3.0 s the force is doubled to 8000 N.

If the car is stopped more quickly, for example by hitting a tree, the stopping time is reduced and the force is further increased.

Car manufacturers use technology to increase stopping time (and distance) to reduce force on the passengers. Reducing force reduces injuries.

Some of the features used are:

- air bags that inflate, stopping passengers more gently

- seat belts that stop passengers hitting hard surfaces inside cars

- crumple zones that collapse steadily in a collision, spreading stopping over a longer time.

When stopping time (and distance) is increased, deceleration is reduced. Injuries are reduced by devices changing shape and absorbing energy.

PROGRESS CHECK

1. Find the momentum of a bicycle and rider of 75 kg travelling at 10 m/s.

2. How does force affect momentum?

3. What is a crumple zone?

4. Define stopping time.

5. How does this affect the passengers?

EXAM QUESTION

a. A trolley of mass 2.0 kg moves with a velocity of 3.0 m/s. Find its momentum.

b. The trolley collides with a stationary trolley of 1.0 kg. The trolleys stick together. Find their combined mass.

c. What is the total momentum of the two trolleys?

d. What is the velocity of the trolleys?

Safe Driving

Driving a car can be a risky business. Many factors can affect the ability of a car to stop.

Stopping Distance

The total **stopping distance** of a car is made up of the **thinking distance** and the **braking distance**.

- Thinking distance = distance travelled between the need for braking occurring and the brakes starting to act.

- Braking distance = distance taken to stop once the brakes have been applied.

Stopping distance = thinking distance + braking distance

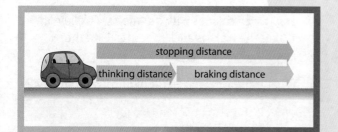

Thinking Distance

The **thinking distance** depends on the driver's reaction time, which can be affected by the following:

- driver tiredness

- influence of alcohol or other drugs

- distractions or lack of concentration.

A greater speed means that a greater distance will be covered in the same time.

If a car is travelling at a speed of 20 m/s and the driver's reaction time is 0.4 s, the thinking distance is:

$$
\begin{aligned}
\text{distance} &= \text{speed} \times \text{time} \\
&= 20\,\text{m/s} \times 0.4\,\text{s} \\
&= 8.0\,\text{m}
\end{aligned}
$$

Braking Distance

The **braking distance** can be affected by the following:

- road conditions – friction is affected when roads are wet or icy

- car conditions – bald tyres, braking force

- mass of car

- speed.

Safe drivers consider the above factors and implications on:

- the distance they are from the car in front

- speed limits.

Active and Passive Safety

Active controls make driving safer, prevent crashes from occurring and better protect occupants during a crash.

Some active safety features are:

- ABS braking. To stop quickly, a car needs a high braking force. This relies on the **friction** between the tyres and the road. If brakes are applied too hard the wheels will lock (stop turning) and the car will begin to skid. ABS braking systems detect this locking and automatically adjust the braking force to prevent skidding.

- Traction control prevents spinning of wheels when excessive acceleration or steering is applied, usually by reducing speed automatically.

- Safety cages.

Some typical **passive** safety features include:

- electric windows
- cruise control
- paddle shift controls on the steering wheel for changing gears or the stereo
- adjustable seating.

Risk

Risks can be expressed in different ways. People make decisions about the amount of risk they are willing to take. Factors that influence people's willingness to accept risks include:

- degree of familiarity
- whether the risk is imposed or voluntary.

Fuel for Cars

The main fuel in road transport is fossil fuels such as petrol and diesel. Electricity can be used for battery-driven cars and solar cars. These do not pollute at point of use, but need battery recharging which uses electricity supplied from power stations.

Fuel consumption depends on:

- speed
- friction
- driving style
- road conditions.

👁 PROGRESS CHECK

1. Define thinking distance.
2. Define braking distance.
3. State **two** factors that affect thinking distance.
4. What is ABS?
5. Name **three** passive safety features in a car.

❓ EXAM QUESTION

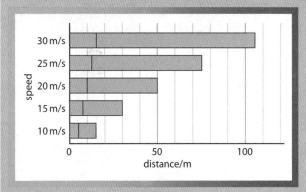

Look at the chart above.

a. At 20 m/s, what is the total stopping distance of a car?

b. At 10 m/s, what is the braking distance of a car?

c. At 10 m/s, what is the thinking distance?

d. State **two** factors that would increase the braking distance.

Energy and Work

Energy and work are both measured in Joules after the physicist James Joule, but they are not quite the same thing.

Transfer of Energy

The scientific meaning of work is the transfer of **energy** from one form to another or from one place to another. A light bulb does work as it changes electrical energy into heat and light. An oven does work as it transfers heat to the food. Therefore, energy is needed to do work.

The law of conservation of energy states that energy can change from one form to another, but it cannot be created or destroyed.

Both energy and work are measured in **Joules** (J).

In this chapter, we will consider **kinetic energy** (KE) and **gravitational potential energy** (PE).

Kinetic energy is found using the equation:

$$\text{kinetic energy} = \frac{1}{2} \times \text{mass} \times \text{velocity}^2$$

$$KE = \frac{1}{2}mv^2$$

All moving objects have kinetic energy. Kinetic energy is greater for objects with:

■ greater speed

■ greater mass.

Doubling the mass doubles the kinetic energy.

Doubling the speed quadruples the kinetic energy. This means that a car with double the speed needs about four times the braking distance.

Potential energy is found using the equation:

> potential energy transferred =
> mass × acceleration of free fall × change in height
>
> PE = mgh

Gravitational potential energy is greater for objects that:

■ are more massive

■ have more height

■ are in a stronger gravitational field.

The acceleration of free fall is sometimes known as gravitational field strength.

Falling Objects

A falling object converts gravitational energy to kinetic energy.

Example

Consider a ball of mass 0.5 kg falling a distance of 15 m.

The potential energy transferred	= mgh
	= 0.5 kg × 10 N/kg × 15 m
	= 75 J

Assuming no energy is lost, all of this energy is converted to kinetic energy.

$$KE = 75\,J = \frac{1}{2}\,mv^2$$

$$\frac{75\,J}{(\frac{1}{2}\,0.5\,kg)} = v^2$$

$$v^2 = 300$$

$$v = 17\,m/s$$

The speed of the ball after falling 15 m will be 17 m/s.

Weight and Work

Weight is the gravitational force from the Earth. It is measured in Newtons and depends on the gravitational field strength, g, which equals about 10 N/kg on Earth.

> Weight = mass × g

An object with mass 20 kg has a weight of 200 N on Earth.

PROGRESS CHECK

1. What is the unit of energy?

2. State the equation to calculate kinetic energy.

3. What is the kinetic energy of a mass of 2.0 kg moving at a velocity of 3 m/s?

4. State the equation to calculate weight.

5. What is the weight on Earth of an object of 4.5 kg?

 EXAM QUESTION

Look at the diagram of a rollercoaster ride.

a. What type of energy is gained as the car moves from point A to point B?

b. Calculate the amount of energy gained if the mass of the car is 100 kg.

c. Assuming all of this energy is converted into kinetic energy as the car moves from B to C, how much kinetic energy does the car have at C?

d. Calculate the maximum speed at point C.

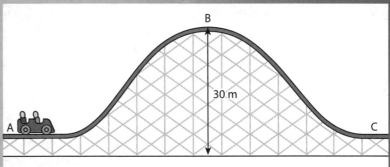

Work and Power

Words such as work and power have special meanings in science and are calculated using specific equations.

Work

Work done is equal to energy transferred; work is done when a force moves an object.

One way of calculating the work done is to use the following equation:

> work done = force × distance moved
> (in the direction of the force)

The amount of work done (Joules) depends on:

- the size of the force in Newtons
- the distance moved in metres.

Work is done and power is developed in:

- lifting weights
- climbing stairs
- pulling a sledge
- pushing a shopping trolley.

The man in the illustration on the right is running up stairs. He is doing work against his weight, the force of gravity. The distance in the direction of this force is the height of the stairs.

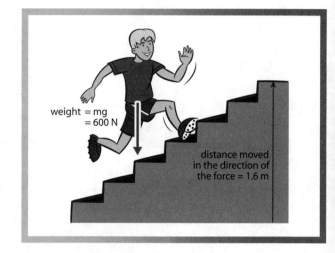

weight = mg
= 600 N

distance moved in the direction of the force = 1.6 m

The work done = force × distance

$$= 600\,N \times 1.6\,m$$

$$= 960\,J$$

He also does some work in the horizontal direction against friction, but this is negligible (small enough to be ignored).

Work done against frictional forces is mainly transformed into heat.

Power is a measurement of how quickly work is being done and is measured in Watts (W).

$$power = \frac{work\ done}{time\ taken}$$

If the man above runs up the stairs in 8.0 s, his power is:

$$\frac{960\,J}{8.0\,s} = 120\,W$$

If he walks up more slowly in 20.0 s, his power is:

$$\frac{960}{20.0\,s} = 48.0\,W$$

The faster work is done, the greater the power.

Elastic Potential and Work

For an object that is able to recover its original shape, elastic potential is the energy stored in the object when work is done to change its shape.

Work Done in Lifting an Object

If an object is lifted a distance of h, the work done is equal to the weight × h:

The weight = mass × g

So the work done in lifting an object: height h = mgh

This is equal to the gain in gravitational potential energy (PE = mgh).

Exam Question

Consider the man below running up the stairs. In this question, the force of friction is ignored.

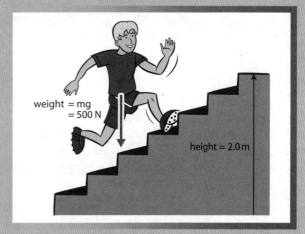

weight = mg = 500 N

height = 2.0 m

a. What force is he working against?

b. Why is the distance of 2.0 m needed rather than the total distance that he moves?

c. Calculate the work that he does running up the stairs.

d. If he runs faster, does he do more work?

Progress Check

1. Define work.

2. What is the unit of work?

3. Give **two** examples of when a person is doing work.

4. What work is done when an object is pushed with a force of 50 N for 2.0 m?

5. What is elastic potential energy?

Inside the Atom

Everything around us including objects, the Earth, the air and even living cells are made of atoms.

An Atom

An atom has a small central **nucleus** composed of **protons** and **neutrons** surrounded by **electrons**.

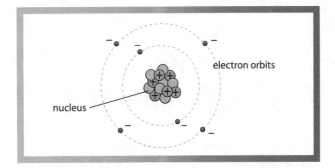

electron orbits

nucleus

Particle	proton	electron	neutron
Charge	+1	−1	none
Mass	1	0	1

The atomic (or proton) number, p, is the number of protons. The mass (or nucleon) number, m, is the number of nucleons (protons + neutrons). For example, an isotope of Radium (Ra) has 226 nucleons, 88 protons and 138 neutrons.

$$_p^m X \qquad _{88}^{226} Ra$$

- Atoms of the same element have the same number of protons.

- Atoms with neutral charge have the same number of electrons as protons.

- An atom may gain or lose electrons to form charged particles called **ions**.

- Atoms with different nucleon numbers have different mass, although they are still the same element. These atoms are called **isotopes**. An isotope of an element has the same number of protons but extra or fewer neutrons.

An unstable nucleus may emit some of its particles. Atoms that give out radiation from their nucleus naturally are said to be **radioactive**.

Alpha radiation is a helium nucleus (2 protons and 2 neutrons). It is emitted straight from the nucleus.

For example, radium decays into radon.

$$_{88}^{226}Ra \rightarrow _{86}^{222}Rn + _2^4 \alpha$$

Beta radiation is an electron emitted from the nucleus. No electrons exist as electrons in the nucleus. However, in an unstable nucleus a neutron may spontaneously change into a proton. When it does this, it emits an electron. This is called beta radiation.

For example, iodine decays into Xenon.

$$_{53}^{128}I \rightarrow _{54}^{128}Xe + _{-1}^0 \beta$$

Gamma radiation is an electromagnetic wave. It usually follows alpha or beta radiation. X-rays have similar properties to gamma rays, but are emitted from different sources.

	Alpha	Beta	Gamma
Range in air	a few centimetres	about a metre	huge distances
Penetration power	stopped by a thick sheet of paper or skin	stopped by a few centimetres of aluminium or other metal	lead or thick concrete will reduce its intensity
Ionising power	strong	weak	very weak
Charge	+2	−1	none

Ionisation is the ability of the radiation to cause other particles to gain or to lose electrons.

PROGRESS CHECK

1. What is the charge on a neutron?

2. Explain how a beta particle can be an electron emitted from a nucleus.

3. What is the range of gamma radiation in air?

4. What is ionisation?

5. What is the ionisation power of alpha radiation?

? EXAM QUESTION

An atom of uranium is written as $^{238}_{92}U$.

a. What is the name given to atoms of the same element with different numbers of neutrons?

b. How many neutrons does each atom of uranium have?

c. The atom emits an alpha particle and decays into thorium (Th). What is the nature of an alpha particle?

d. Write an equation for this decay.

Radiation and Science

Throughout history, scientific ideas and theories about radiation have been changed and developed as new discoveries are made.

Some theories, such as Einstein's theory of relativity, do not originate from experiments. Einstein used his imagination and carried out thought experiments.

Einstein's theory led to predictions that were tested successfully. These tests involved atomic clocks and cosmic rays. The results agreed with the theory and led to more people accepting the ideas.

Without testing new theories, scientists are often reluctant to accept them, especially when they overturn long-established explanations.

Another example of a new theory is 'cold fusion'. Usually fusion requires extremely high temperatures and densities. Theories such as 'cold fusion' are not accepted until they have been validated by the scientific community.

The Plum Pudding Model

Scientists used to believe that atoms were the smallest particles that existed. In 1897, J. J. Thompson discovered tiny, negatively charged particles which he named electrons. Thompson found that atoms sometimes give out electrons. Since the overall charge of an atom is neutral, Thomson deduced that an atom might consist of a sphere of positively charged mass with negative electrons inside it. This model of the atom is known as the 'plum pudding' model since the electrons look a little bit like plums in a pudding.

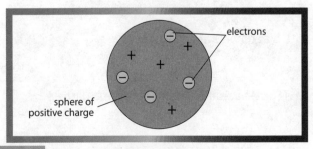

electrons

sphere of positive charge

The Nuclear Model

The scientist Ernest Rutherford had two assistants, Hans Geiger and Ernest Marsden. In 1911 Rutherford asked them to carry out a new experiment to discover more about atoms.

In the experiment, a thin piece of gold foil was bombarded with alpha particles. Gold foil was chosen because it is very thin. Alpha particles are tiny positive particles emitted by some radioactive substances.

Rutherford found that nearly all of the alpha particles went straight through the gold leaf. Very, very few of the alpha particles were deflected by the atoms in the foil!

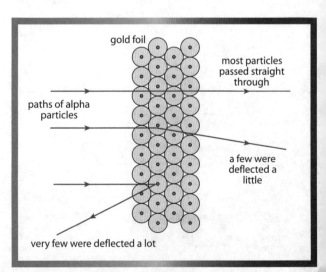

gold foil

most particles passed straight through

paths of alpha particles

a few were deflected a little

very few were deflected a lot

Rutherford concluded that:

- most of an atom is empty space

- most of the mass of an atom is compressed into a tiny volume in the centre called a nucleus

- the nucleus of an atom has an overall positive charge.

Rutherford's new nuclear model of the atom proposed that tiny negatively charged electrons orbited around a dense positive nucleus. The diagram below shows the nucleus many times larger than it would be if the diagram were to scale.

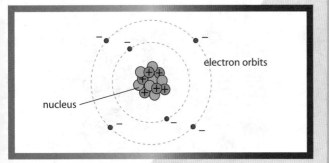

PROGRESS CHECK

1. How does testing a model change the way scientists think about it?

2. Give an example of a recent model that needs testing.

3. What particle did Thompson discover?

4. Why is Thompson's model called the 'plum pudding'?

5. What extra information do we know about electrons today?

Modern Models

Other scientists have refined Rutherford's model with the discovery of neutrons and energy levels for the electrons. Scientists recently discovered that electrons can behave like clouds of charge, or even waves. Today, scientists use a mathematical model of an atom using wave mechanics.

? EXAM QUESTION

This question is about the Rutherford model of the atom.

a. What particles did Rutherford bombard the gold with in his experiment?

b. Why did he use gold foil?

c. What happened to most of the particles?

d. What were the main conclusions of his experiment?

Safe Radiation

Radiation can damage or destroy living cells due to its ionising power. It is important to ensure that people exposed to radiation are kept safe.

Radiation

Radiation can cause cancer or make vital organs stop working. High levels of radiation pose a greater risk. Over time, scientists have learnt more about the risks associated with radioactive sources.

Background radiation is a low level of radiation that is around us all of the time. It is mainly caused by natural radioactive substances such as rocks, soil, living things and cosmic rays. Humans also contribute to background radiation, for example medical uses, nuclear waste and power stations.

The Earth's atmosphere and magnetic field protect it from radiation from space. The ozone layer protects the Earth from ultraviolet radiation, but pollution from CFCs is depleting the layer.

Different regions in the UK experience different levels of background radiation. A main cause of this variation is radon gas in the atmosphere.

Nuclear Power

Radioactive fuel rods release energy as heat through a process called **nuclear fission**. A nuclear power station uses this heat to drive turbines and generate electricity.

Nuclear power stations pose two main risks:

- accidental emission of radioactive material
- waste material disposal.

A radioactive leak could cause damage to humans and wildlife for many years. Radioactive dust can be carried by the wind for thousands of kilometres.

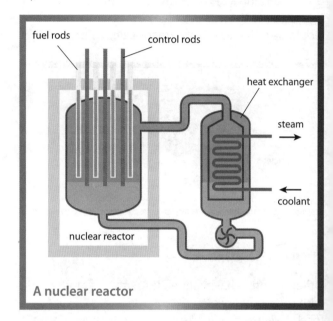

A nuclear reactor

Here are some general risks associated with radiation:

- Alpha radiation is highly ionising and very dangerous if it is taken into the body. It cannot pass through the skin. However, if it is absorbed in food or by breathing in radioactive gas or dust, the radiation can cause damage deep inside the body.

- Beta and gamma rays can penetrate the skin but most sources of these radiations are well shielded, such as power stations and laboratories.

- Some media reports claim that microwave radiation from mobile phones or masts poses a health risk.

Safety in the Laboratory

Radioactive substances must be handled safely in the laboratory.

- Tongs or gloves must be used.

- The exposure time must be minimised.

- Sources should be stored in shielded containers.

- Protective clothing must be worn.

PROGRESS CHECK

1. State **three** sources of background radiation.

2. Is the radiation from mobile phones dangerous?

3. Give a reason why alpha radioactive dust is very dangerous.

4. Can alpha radiation penetrate the skin?

5. Can gamma radiation penetrate the skin?

EXAM QUESTION

a. What is the name of the radioactive process that takes place in a nuclear power station?

b. State **two** dangers associated with nuclear power stations.

c. How is the Earth protected from radiation from space?

d. Give **two** precautions that should be taken when handling radioactive sources in a laboratory.

Nuclear Power

Nuclear power stations produce much more energy than coal or oil fired power stations and they emit no greenhouse gases that might contribute to global warming.

Nuclear Fission

Einstein suggested the possibility of releasing enormous amounts of energy trapped in an atom from his relation between mass and energy. **Fission** is the **splitting** of an atom into two lighter nuclei.

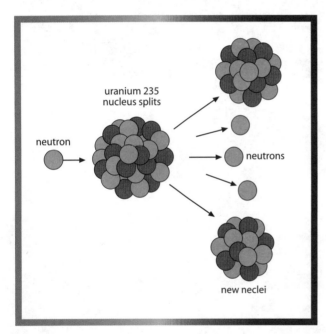

uranium 235
nucleus splits

neutron

neutrons

new neclei

The process:

- The atom (usually uranium 235) is bombarded with a neutron that is initially absorbed.

- This makes the nucleus highly unstable.

- The nucleus splits into two lighter nuclei (daughter nuclei) and releases two or three neutrons.

- The neutrons bombard other nuclei causing further splitting.

- Energy is released rapidly.

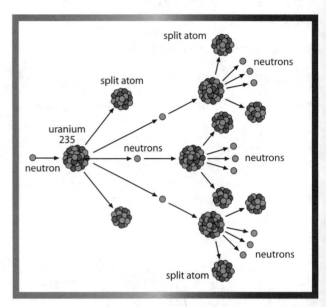

split atom

neutrons

split atom

uranium 235

neutrons

neutron

neutrons

neutrons

split atom

This is known as a **chain reaction**. If the chain reaction is **uncontrolled** the thermal energy is released extremely rapidly, resulting in an explosion or nuclear bomb.

Nuclear Power

In a nuclear reactor, fission is controlled.

- A moderator such as graphite or water slows down the neutrons.

- Control rods (that can be raised or lowered) absorb some neutrons but leave enough to keep the reaction going.

Radioactive fuel rods such as uranium 235 or plutonium 239 release energy as heat through nuclear fission. In the pressurised reactor on the right, the hot water is used to produce steam. Steam turns a turbine which drives a generator to produce electricity.

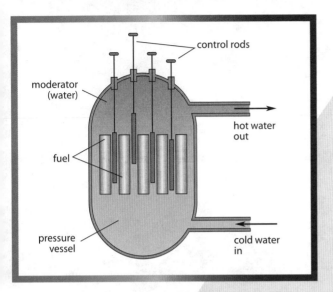

Some of the advantages of nuclear power are:

- It does not contribute to global warming.
- It produces high stocks of fuel (non-renewable).
- Small amounts of fuel give large amounts of energy (about a million times more than that from burning).

Some disadvantages are:

- It has high maintenance costs.
- It has high decommissioning (closing down) costs.
- There is a risk of accidental emission of radioactive material.
- It creates radioactive waste.

Radioactive Waste

After a few years, the fuel in a reactor must be replaced. The used fuel consists of dangerous radioactive products that need to be stored safely for up to thousands of years. Materials that are near radioactive sources or inside a nuclear reactor absorb extra neutrons, making them radioactive too.

Low level radioactive waste can be buried in landfill sites. Other waste must be encased in thick glass or concrete and buried. Some types of waste can be reprocessed.

Some problems of dealing with radioactive waste are:

- It can cause cancer if not disposed of correctly.
- It can remain radioactive for thousands of years.
- Plutonium (waste product from nuclear reactors) can be used to make bombs and could be considered a terrorist risk.
- It must be kept out of groundwater.

Nuclear Fusion

Nuclear fusion is the joining of two atomic nuclei to form a larger one. It is the energy source for stars. It is an impractical source of energy due to the extremely high temperatures and densities it requires.

PROGRESS CHECK

1. In a chain reaction a particle is split. What are the products?
2. What does the name 'daughter nuclei' refer to?
3. How can nuclear waste be disposed of?
4. How long can nuclear waste remain radioactive for?
5. What is nuclear fusion?

EXAM QUESTION

This question is about a nuclear power station.

a. What is a moderator?

b. What are the control rods?

c. State **two** advantages of nuclear power.

d. State **two** disadvantages of nuclear power.

Radiation Issues

Radiation is very useful and has improved the quality of human life in areas such as medicine and industry.

Some Uses of Radiation

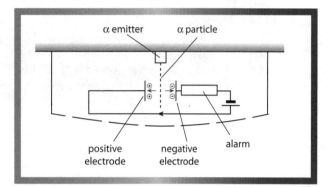

Alpha radiation is used in smoke alarms. Beta or gamma radiation can be used as tracers in industry and for diagnostic purposes in hospitals.

- In hospitals a tracer is swallowed or injected into the body. It is followed on the outside by a radiation detector. This method is used to check a patient's thyroid gland.

- In industry tracers are used in underground pipes. A gamma source is normally used so it can penetrate to the surface. The source is tracked by a detector above ground. A leak or a blockage is shown by a reduction in the activity.

- Gamma radiation is used to treat food so it keeps longer.

- Gamma radiation is used to sterilise equipment.

- Gamma rays are used to treat cancer. A wide beam is focused on the tumour and rotated around the person with the tumour at the centre. This limits the damage to non-cancerous tissue. Radiation with the least penetrating effect possible and the shortest possible half-life also minimises exposure.

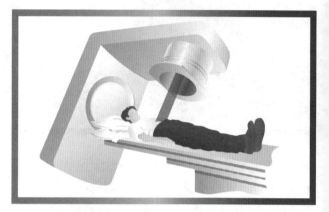

Half-life

The radioactivity (or activity) of an isotope is the number of decays emitted per second. It decreases over time.

The half-life of a radioactive sample is defined as the time it takes for the number of undecayed nuclei to halve. It can also be defined as the time it takes for the count rate (activity) to halve. The half-life for any sample is always constant.

A sample with a half-life of 2 days will be half its original value in 2 days, a quarter in 4 days and so on.

The half-life can be used to date artefacts in archaeology and rocks. Archaeologists assume that the amount of carbon 14 has not changed in the air for thousands of years. When an object (e.g. tree) dies, gaseous exchange with the air stops. The Carbon 14 in the wood decays and the ratio of activity from living matter to the sample leads to a reasonably accurate date. Radioactive dating of rocks depends on the uranium to lead ratio. Scientific conclusions, such as those from radioactive dating, often carry significant uncertainties.

X-rays

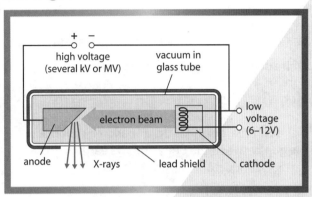

A radiographer is a person who takes X-rays. X-rays and gamma rays have similar wavelengths but are produced in different ways. Gamma rays are given out from the nucleus of certain radioactive materials. X-rays are made by firing high speed electrons at metal targets and are easier to control than gamma rays.

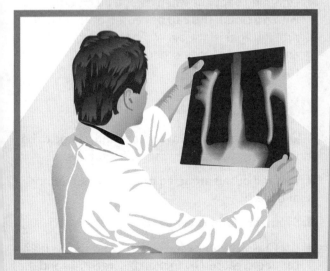

PROGRESS CHECK

1. Suggest a use for alpha radiation.

2. Suggest an industrial use for a tracer.

3. When treating cancer, why is a wide beam of gamma radiation focused on the tumour?

4. What is the difference between X-rays and gamma rays?

5. State an advantage of using X-rays instead of gamma rays.

EXAM QUESTION

1. Define half-life.

2. A sample has an activity of 400 counts per second. After three days the activity is 200 counts per second. What is the half-life?

3. What will the activity be after nine days?

4. What do archaeologists try to calculate using the half-life of Carbon 14?

Static Electricity

Static electricity or **charge** is caused by **electrons** – tiny, negative particles around the nucleus of atoms.

When some materials are rubbed together, electrons can be transferred from one material to the other.

- A build up of electrons creates a negative charge.
- A lack of electrons creates a positive charge.

You may have experienced static charge when combing your hair. If the comb is made of polythene, it may gain electrons from your hair, leaving your hair positive and the comb negative. Positive and negative charges attract so the comb attracts your hair.

Hair will gain electrons from an acetate comb, leaving the comb positive and your hair negative. Again, the opposite charges will attract.

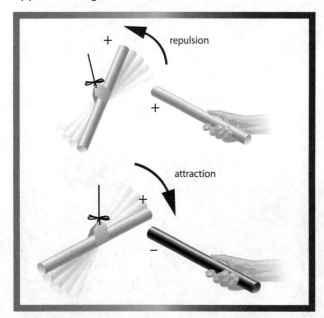

repulsion

attraction

Objects that have the same charge will repel.

Insulated materials can be charged by the transfer of electrons. If an object is connected to the ground by a conducting material, the charge flows away.

- **Conductor** – charge (electrons) can pass through.
- **Insulator** – charge cannot pass through.

When Static is Dangerous

If enough charge builds up, a spark may jump across the gap between the body and the earth or an earthed conductor.

- Aircraft fuel causes static as the fuel rubs against the pipe. A spark could ignite the fuel vapour. The aircraft and the tanker are earthed to avoid the charge building up.
- Lorries with inflammable gases and liquids are earthed before unloading.
- Lightning happens when charge builds up within a cloud. This can be caused by ice particles rubbing against the air. When the charge is large enough it leaps to another part of the cloud, or to the ground.

When Static is a Nuisance

These situations do not involve enough charge to be dangerous. However, they can be a nuisance.

- Dirt and dust is attracted to TV screens, monitors and plastic.
- Synthetic clothing clings.
- Cars are sometimes earthed to avoid shocks from car doors, caused by friction between you and the car.
- After walking across a floor covered with insulating material you may experience a shock if you touch water pipes or some other earthed conductor.

Preventing Static Electricity

Some ways to prevent static shocks are:

- correct earthing
- insulating mats
- wearing rubber-soled shoes
- use of anti-static sprays.

Uses of Static Electricity

- Paint spraying – paint is charged so that the droplets repel each other, giving a fine, even spray. A surface is given an opposite charge to the paint, ensuring an even coat and less waste.

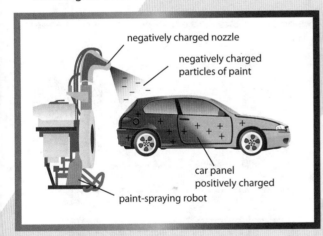

negatively charged nozzle

negatively charged particles of paint

car panel positively charged

paint-spraying robot

- Photocopiers and laser printers use static to direct ink.

- Dust can be removed from chimneys by being attracted to a charged plate. Large particles form, falling when they are heavy enough or shaken.

- Finger printing uses static electricity.

- Some dusters are designed to attract dust by static electricity.

- Doctors use static electricity to restart the heart.

 PROGRESS CHECK

1. Define an electrical conductor.

2. Define an electrical insulator.

3. Why is an aircraft earthed when refuelling?

4. How can static be prevented?

5. Give an example of when static electricity can be a nuisance.

EXAM QUESTION

A painter makes use of static electricity when spray painting a surface.

a. Why does charging the paint produce a fine, even spray?

b. Should the surface be charged with the same charge to the paint?

c. What effect will this have?

d. Suggest another use of static electricity.

Electricity on the Move I

When electrons move through a conductor, they carry charge. This flow of charge is what we know as electric current.

Electric Current

Electric **current** is the movement of charge through a conductor. Current is measured in **Amps** or Amperes – it is equal to the amount of charge that flows every second. The unit of charge is the Coulomb (C).

This equation relates the amount of electrical charge that flows to current and time.

charge = current × time

The charged particles that flow in a wire are electrons that have a **negative charge**. They flow from negative to positive. Ions are positive particles left behind when the electrons move. We say that electric current is the flow of **positively** charged ions from positive to negative but ions don't actually move.

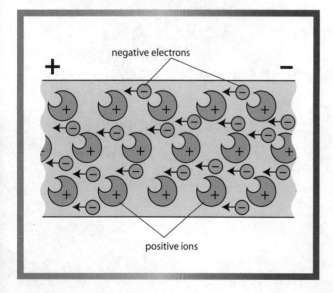

Providing a Potential Difference

Cells produce a flow of charge when a conducting wire is connected from the positive terminal of the cell to the negative terminal. The charge flows due to the **potential difference** between the terminals. Potential difference is measured in volts – sometimes called **voltage**. The flow of current from a cell is always in one direction, and is called **direct current** or **DC**. A battery is a number of cells connected together in series.

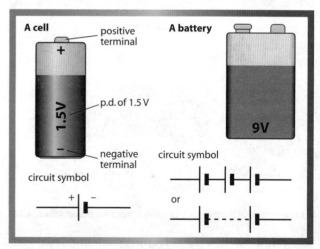

The mains supplies a potential difference of 220 V. The current supplied by the mains is called **alternating current** or **AC** because it continuously changes direction.

Energy

When electrical charge flows through a resistor, electrical **energy** is transformed into heat energy and the resistor heats up.

Energy transformed, potential difference and charge are related by the following equation.

energy transformed = potential difference × charge

In order for a current to flow, a complete loop is required.

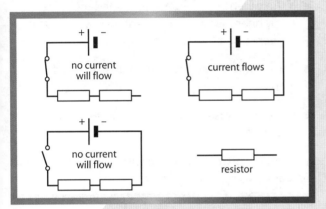

Current is measured using an ammeter. The ammeter must be placed in series (next to) any other components. The current is the same at all points in a series circuit so it can be placed either side of the component.

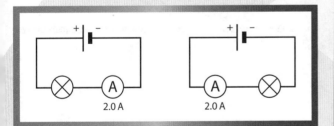

Measuring Potential Difference

Potential difference is measured using a voltmeter. The voltmeter must be placed in parallel with the component that it is measuring.

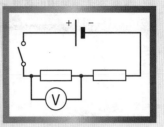

PROGRESS CHECK

1. How is current defined?

2. Are the following statements true or false?

   a. Electrons have a negative charge.

   b. Electrons flow from positive to negative.

   c. Ions flow from positive to negative.

   d. Current is said to flow from positive to negative.

EXAM QUESTION

a. In the circuit on the right, electricity flows from positive to negative. Add arrows to the circuit to show the direction of current flow.

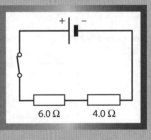

b. Add an ammeter to the circuit to measure the current through the resistors.

c. Add a voltmeter that will measure the potential difference across the 4.0 Ω resistor.

d. What will happen if the switch is opened?

Electricity on the Move 2

Resistance is how we measure how easy or difficult it is for electricity to flow through a material.

Current passes easily through copper wire because it has a low **resistance**. Current does not pass so easily through a filament lamp, however. The filament lamp has a higher **resistance**. More energy is needed to push the electrons through the filament wire in the lamp. This energy is converted to heat (and light) in the lamp. Components with a higher resistance give off more heat.

Calculating Resistance

Resistance is measured in Ohms (Ω). The resistance of a component is found using the following equation:

$$\text{resistance} = \frac{\text{potential difference}}{\text{current}}$$

- Resistance in Ohms (Ω)

- Potential difference (voltage) in Volts (V)

- Current in Amps (A)

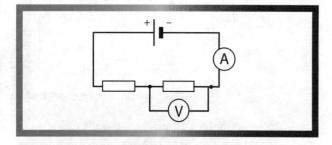

There is a potential difference across this component of 12.0 V and a current through it of 3.0 A.

$$\text{Resistance} = \frac{12.0\,\text{V}}{3.0\,\text{A}} = 4.0\ \Omega.$$

- If the potential difference remained the same, a component with a higher resistance would have a *lower* current passing through it.

- If the potential difference remained the same, a component with a lower resistance would have a *higher* current passing through it.

- For a given resistor, current increases as p.d. increases.

- For a given resistor, current decreases as p.d. decreases.

A **variable resistor** is a device with a control to vary its resistance. Its symbol is:

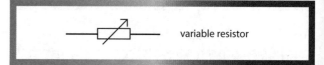
variable resistor

In **series**, the total resistance equals the sum of the individual resistances.

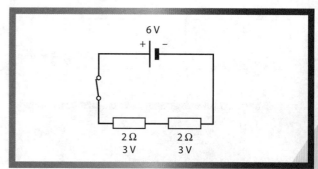

- There is the same current in each component.

- The p.d. of the supply is shared by the components.

In **parallel**, the total resistance is less than each of the individual resistors.

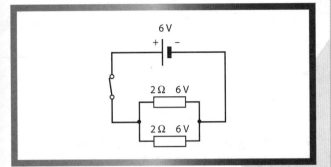

■ The p.d. across each component is the same.

■ The current is shared by the components.

Power and Energy

The rate at which energy is transferred in a device is called the **power**.

$$\text{power} = \text{current} \times \text{voltage}$$

This equation can be used to determine the size of fuse a device needs (see page 116 for more on fuses). For example, a kettle with a power of 2000 W uses mains voltage of 220 V.

$$\text{current} = \frac{2000\,\text{W}}{220\,\text{V}} = 9.1\,\text{A}$$

The current of a fuse needs to be above this, so this appliance needs a 10 A fuse.

Electrical energy can be calculated using the equation:

$$\text{energy} = \text{voltage} \times \text{current} \times \text{time}$$

(see page 116 for more on fuses)

PROGRESS CHECK

1. Find the resistance of a component with a p.d. of 6.0 V and a current of 4.0 A.

2. A resistor is replaced with a resistor of higher resistance. How will the current in the circuit change?

3. What is the circuit symbol for a variable resistor?

4. What current is drawn by a vacuum cleaner of power 900 W and voltage 220 V?

5. Suggest a suitable fuse for the vacuum cleaner.

EXAM QUESTION

In the following circuit, the resistors each have resistance of 5 Ω.

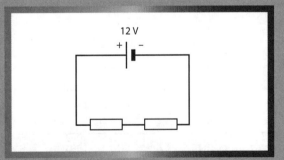

a. What is the total resistance?

b. What is the current through each resistor?

c. What is the p.d. across each resistor?

d. How could both resistors be arranged so that the total resistance is less than 5 Ω?

Using Electricity

In our homes, many appliances use electricity. When we have an electricity cut we realise how much we rely on electricity.

Plugs

A plug has three wires: live, neutral and earth.

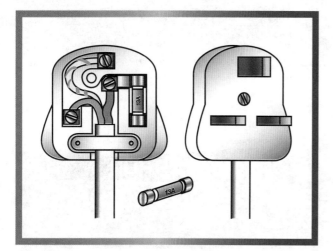

	Colour	Function
Live	brown	alternating between positive and negative voltage
Neutral	blue	completes the circuit, stays at zero voltage
Earth	green/yellow	safety wire

Safe electricity

Too much current in a wire causes overheating and can cause a fire.

Some ways of improving safety when using electricity are:

- A **fuse** is a short piece of thin wire placed in a circuit that melts with high current, breaking the circuit. The live wire must be connected through the fuse.

- **Residual current circuit breakers** (RCCBs) improve the safety of a device by disconnecting a circuit automatically whenever it detects that the flow of current is too high.

- An earth wire is a safety wire that connects the metal parts of a device to earth and stops the device becoming dangerous to touch if there is a loose wire. If a wire works loose and touches a metal part of the device a large current flows to earth, blowing the fuse or activating the circuit breaker.

- Many modern devices are insulated with a plastic case which insulates the user from any wiring faults. Since the wires themselves are also insulated, this is known as **double insulation**.

Changing Resistance

The resistance of some components is constant. The resistance of other components can change.

- The resistance of a **filament lamp** increases with more current, the lamp gets hotter. The symbol for a lamp is:

- A **light dependent resistor** (LDR) has a *high* resistance in the dark and a *low* resistance in the light. It is used to detect light or switch a lamp on automatically in the dark.

light dependent resistor (LDR)

- A **thermistor** has a **high** resistance when cold and a **low** resistance when hot. It is used to detect temperature change for a fire alarm.

thermistor

- The current through a **diode** flows in one direction only. It has a very high resistance in the reverse direction.

diode

Graphs

If potential difference is plotted on the y-axis and current on the x-axis, the gradient is equal to the resistance. For a component with a constant resistance, for example, a resistor at constant temperature, the gradient is constant.

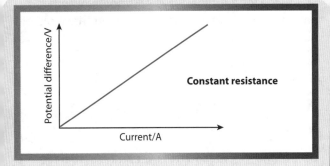

In a filament lamp the gradient increases as current increases because the resistance increases as temperature increases.

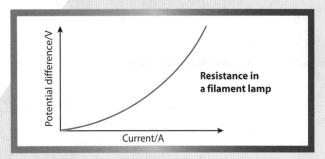

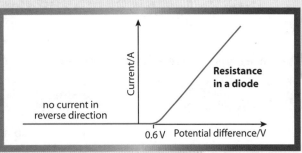

PROGRESS CHECK

1. What is the symbol for an LDR?
2. Explain how the resistance of a filament lamp changes with current.
3. What does the graph look like for a component with constant resistance?
4. A thermistor is placed in a beaker of crushed ice. What happens to its resistance?
5. Suggest a use for a thermistor.

EXAM QUESTION

1. In a plug, what must the live wire be connected through?
2. How is someone using a hairdryer protected by the use of an earth wire and a fuse?
3. What is an RCCB?
4. A hairdryer that is double insulated does not require an earth wire. Why not?

Waves

Waves transmit energy from one place to another either through space or through a material.

Transverse and Longitudinal Waves

The wave equation states that for any wave:

$$speed = frequency \times wavelength$$

- **Frequency** is the number of waves passing a point per second and is measured in Hertz (Hz).

- **Wavelength** is the distance between any point on a wave and the same point on the next wave.

- **Amplitude** is the maximum displacement of the waves from rest position.

There are two types of wave, **transverse** and **longitudinal**. Transverse waves vibrate with a displacement **perpendicular** to the direction of travel of the wave. Examples are electromagnetic waves (including light) and water waves.

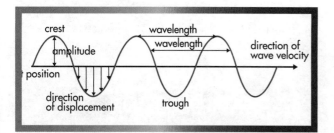

Longitudinal waves vibrate with a displacement **parallel** to the direction of travel of the wave. Examples are sound waves and seismic waves.

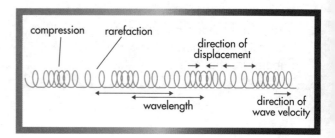

When sound travels through air, the particles vibrate backwards and forwards, parallel to the direction of the wave.

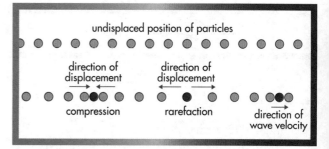

Ultrasound

Sound is a longitudinal wave. Ultrasound waves have a higher frequency than the upper threshold of human hearing. Ultrasound is used to:

- look inside people (body scans); it reflects at layer boundaries

- break down kidney and other stones

- measure the speed of blood flow.

Ultrasound has advantages over X-rays in that it:

- can produce images of soft tissue

- does not damage living cells.

Alternating Current

Direct current is electricity produced by cells and batteries. It travels in one direction only. Alternating current produces electricity that flows backwards and forwards, in a transverse wave shape. This can be observed on an oscilloscope. Mains electricity is an a.c. supply with a frequency of 50 cycles per second (50Hz).

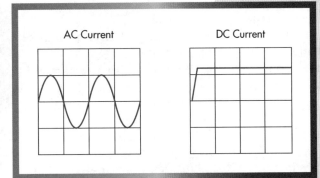

AC Current

DC Current

PROGRESS CHECK

1. Define wavelength.

2. Define amplitude.

3. Which types of waves have compressions and rarefactions?

4. Which types of waves have peaks and troughs?

5. Is electricity a wave?

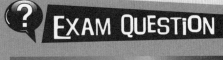

? EXAM QUESTION

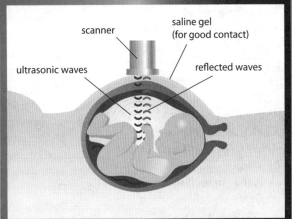

saline gel (for good contact)

scanner

ultrasonic waves

reflected waves

a. Human ears can detect sound waves of frequency up to about 20 000 Hz. Give a possible frequency of ultrasound.

b. Name **one** use of ultrasound.

c. Why is it preferable to use ultrasound when scanning an unborn baby?

d. Name **one** other advantage of ultrasound over X-rays.

Answers

Biology

Day 1

pages 4–5
How Science Works
PROGRESS CHECK
1. The variable we choose to change in an experiment
2. The variable that we measure in an experiment
3. A variable that can be put in order
4. A variable that can have any whole number value
5. Close to the true value
EXAM QUESTION
a. The force applied
b. The length of the spring
c. Using the same spring, etc.

pages 6–7
Cells
PROGRESS CHECK
1. Respiration
2. A cell that has changed its shape to perform a particular function
3. Cells that have the ability to replicate and differentiate into different types of tissue throughout the life of the organism
EXAM QUESTION
1. Chloroplast, cell wall
2. Contain chlorophyll to absorb light for photosynthesis

pages 8–9
Diffusion and Osmosis
PROGRESS CHECK
1. The movement of particles from an area of high concentration to an area of low concentration
2. Water

3. They have no cell wall
EXAM QUESTION
1. a. Carbon dioxide into the leaf; oxygen and water vapour out of the leaf
   b. Glucose and oxygen into cells; waste materials out of cells; the exchange of carbon dioxide and oxygen at the lungs
2. Thin walled – less diffusion distance; lots of them – large surface area; close contact with blood capillaries – short diffusion distance; blood takes oxygen away – sets up a concentration gradient

pages 10–11
Enzymes and Nutrition
PROGRESS CHECK
1. Temperature, pH
2. In biological washing powders to digest protein stains; used to predigest protein in baby foods
3. Carbohydrase
EXAM QUESTION
a. For a fair test; to enable a comparison to be made
b. Catalase/enzyme in liver more effective; liver contains more enzyme; conditions favoured the liver enzymes

pages 12–13
The Environment
PROGRESS CHECK
1. Pyramid of numbers
2. Pyramid of biomass
3. Factors that affect the rate of photosynthesis
EXAM QUESTION
1. a. Carbon dioxide, b. glucose
2. Amount of light, amount of CO_2,

temperature
3. flat and thin – large surface area for absorbing sunlight; thin so CO_2 can reach the cells easily; stomata on lower surface for gas exchange by diffusion; veins to carry substances to and from the leaf; chloroplasts with chlorophyll concentrated near upper surface to absorb sunlight

pages 14–15
Interactions in Environments
PROGRESS CHECK
1. When organisms interact and rely on each other to live
2. To indicate the presence or absence of pollution
3. The chopping down of trees
EXAM QUESTION
a. Bacteria use hydrogen sulfide and oxygen to make energy instead of light. Proteins in their body can withstand the high temperatures
b. High altitudes, extreme temperatures
c. Photosynthesis uses light; chemosynthesis uses chemicals to make energy

pages 16–17
Cycles
PROGRESS CHECK
1. Photosynthesis
2. Respiration and burning
3. Making proteins
EXAM QUESTION
1. and 2.
   Denitrifying bacteria – change nitrates into ammonia and then nitrogen gas; nitrogen fixing bacteria – convert nitrogen

gas into nitrates; nitrifying bacteria – change ammonia into nitrates.

pages 18–19
Respiration and Exercise
PROGRESS CHECK
1. The breakdown of glucose to make energy using oxygen
2. The incomplete breakdown of glucose forming lactic acid and a small amount of energy
3. The amount of oxygen needed to remove/break down lactic acid formed by anaerobic respiration

EXAM QUESTION
a. Athlete A
b. The recovery rate was quicker/ got back to resting rate sooner; lower starting pulse rate; lower pulse rate during exercise
c. Heart rate monitors; takes a continuous measurement, less chance of human error

pages 20–21
Homeostasis
PROGRESS CHECK
1. Maintaining a constant internal environment
2. The pancreas not making enough insulin
3. The pancreas

EXAM QUESTION
a. Vasoconstriction of blood vessels; shivering; no sweat; increased respiration
b. Hypothalamus
c. 37°C

Day 2

pages 22–23
Excretion and Homeostasis
PROGRESS CHECK
1. The exchange of carbon dioxide and oxygen between the lungs and the blood

2. Lots of them; close contact with blood; moist; thin membrane
3. The control of the amount of water in the body

EXAM QUESTION
a. Liver; from excess amino acids
b. Urea is forced out of the blood in the nephron at high pressure and forms urine; urine travels down the ureter to the bladder
c. Excess ions/salts and water

pages 24–25
Mitosis
PROGRESS CHECK
1. 2
2. 46
3. DNA

EXAM QUESTION
1. a. True, b. false, c. true
2. Occurs in the growth and replacement of cells, where the chromosome number has to stay the same

pages 26–27
Meiosis
PROGRESS CHECK
1. Zygote
2. 23
3. Female

EXAM QUESTION
1. a. Meiosis, b. mitosis, c. meiosis
2. Fertilisation

pages 28–29
Genes
PROGRESS CHECK
1. A section of DNA that codes for a particular protein or enzyme
2. 46
3. In the nucleus, then in the cytoplasm on ribosomes

EXAM QUESTION
1. Double helix; two strands coiled; joined by four bases like the rungs of a ladder
2. Genes are a section of DNA, chromosomes are made of DNA

3. DNA unwinds to expose a sequence of bases (genes) that are copied by mRNA and then formed into a protein during protein synthesis

pages 30–31
Manipulating Life
PROGRESS CHECK
1. Asexual reproduction
2. Clones of each other but not their parents
3. A technique to correct defective genes responsible for diseases by replacing abnormal genes with normal genes

EXAM QUESTION
a. False, if it involves sexual reproduction
b. Cuttings or tissue culture
c. It always involves sexual reproduction, which produces variation

pages 32–33
Inheritance and Disease
PROGRESS CHECK
1. Having two of the same alleles
2. By inheriting two recessive alleles
3. Onset of the disease is late; sufferers may have already had children and passed it on; only one allele needed to inherit disease so 50% chance

EXAM QUESTION
a.

	R	r
R	RR	Rr
r	Rr	rr

b. RR or Rr – tongue rollers; rr – non-tongue rollers

pages 34–35
Food Production
PROGRESS CHECK
1. Less exercise means more chance of weight gain
2. Fish farming/battery hens
3. Hydroponics/greenhouse

EXAM QUESTION
Advantages of organic farming –
leaves countryside alone; kinder to
animals; uses organic manure; no
chemicals (any two)
Disadvantages – expensive as
labour intensive; uses up more land
space
Advantages of intensive farming
– produces more food in a smaller
area; lower labour costs means
cheaper food; can be used to
improve stocks that are in danger,
i.e. fish farming (any two)
Disadvantages – can be expensive
because of use of antibiotics and
keeping animals warm; can be
unkind to animals; worry that
antibiotics could get into food
chains (any two)

pages 36–37
Plant Hormones
PROGRESS CHECK
1. Auxin
2. Slows down
3. Speeds up
EXAM QUESTION
a. Less chance of damage in
   storage; last longer; easier to
   pick
b. Plant hormones
c. Growing cuttings; producing
   seedless fruits; killing weeds

pages 38–39
Plant Growth
PROGRESS CHECK
1. To make proteins
2. Stunted growth, yellow older
   leaves
3. Dissolved in water; active
   transport to root hairs; xylem
   tubes transport them to the leaves
EXAM QUESTION
1. Elongation/enlargement
   in plants is the main way
   plants gain height; animals

stop growing, plants grow
continually; cell division in
plants only takes place at the
root and shoot tips; plant cells
retain the ability to differentiate
throughout life, animals lose
this ability (any two)
2. Space; climate; availability of
   nutrients; inheritance of genes
3. Root and shoot tips

Day 3
pages 40–41
Animal Growth
PROGRESS CHECK
1. Genes, nutrition, hormones
2. Mitosis and differentiation
3. The ability to re-grow parts of
   the body
EXAM QUESTION
1. a. Infancy, childhood, puberty,
      maturity, old age
   b. The limit to the number of
      times a cell can divide
   c. Malignant cancer cells, stem
      cells

pages 42–43
The Circulatory System
PROGRESS CHECK
1. Arteries
2. To withstand high pressure
3. To prevent the backflow of
   blood
EXAM QUESTION
1. Small biconcave disc – more
   surface area to volume ratio;
   no nucleus – more room for
   haemoglobin; small and flexible
   – able to pass through capillary
   walls
2. White blood cells, platelets,
   plasma containing many
   dissolved substances
3. In blood vessels; pumped
   around the body by the heart

Chemistry
pages 44–45
Atomic Structure
PROGRESS CHECK
1. They have the same number of
   protons
2. Nucleus
3. Electrons
4. In a periodic table
5. 100
EXAM QUESTION
a. 6 protons, 6 electrons and 7
   neutrons
b. Mass of 1 and a charge of 1+

pages 46–47
Electronic Structure
PROGRESS CHECK
1. Shells/levels
2. Two
3. 2,1
4. Protons and neutrons
5. Group 3/III
EXAM QUESTION
a. 2,8,2
b. Group 2

pages 48–49
Ionic Bonding
PROGRESS CHECK
1. An atom or group of atoms with
   a charge
2. 1–
3. 1+
4. 2–
5. 2+
EXAM QUESTION
a. It has lots of strong ionic bonds
b. sodium + chlorine → sodium
   chloride
c. 1+

pages 50–51
Covalent Bonding
PROGRESS CHECK
1. H_2
2. HCl
3. CH_4
4. NH_3
5. O_2

EXAM QUESTION

a. A shared pair of electrons

b. H_2O

c. Although there are strong bonds within the water molecules there are only weak forces of attraction between one molecule and the next

pages 52–53
Alkali Metals
PROGRESS CHECK

1. On the left-hand side
2. Potassium
3. Hydrogen
4. Orange
5. Lilac

EXAM QUESTION

a. sodium + water → sodium hydroxide + hydrogen
b. $2Na + 2H_2O \rightarrow 2NaOH + H_2$
c. So it does not react with air or water
d. The outer electron is further from the nucleus so it is lost more easily

Day 4

pages 54–55
Noble Gases and Halogens
PROGRESS CHECK

1. Halogens/Group 7
2. Noble gases/Group 0
3. Liquid
4. Balloons
5. Filament lamps

EXAM QUESTION

a. halogens/Group 7
b. chlorine + potassium iodide → potassium chloride + iodine

pages 56–57
Calculations
PROGRESS CHECK

1. To compare the mass of different atoms
2. Carbon -12
3. The relative formula mass of a substance in grams

4. It does not go to completion
5. The percentage yield of a reaction = actual amount of product / theoretical yield × 100%

EXAM QUESTION

a. The reaction is reversible and does not go to completion/ some of the product was lost, for example, during filtering or evaporation/there may be side-reactions which are producing another product
b. 88%

pages 58–59
Haber Process
PROGRESS CHECK

1. Fractional distillation of liquid air
2. Natural gas
3. Iron
4. Around 450 °C
5. Around 200 atmospheres

EXAM QUESTION

a. To make protein
b. Nitric acid
c. 82%

pages 60–61
Rates of Reaction
PROGRESS CHECK

1. They need to collide and when they do collide they must have enough energy to react (activation energy)
2. Increases the rate of reaction
3. Decreases the rate of reaction
4. Increases the rate of reaction
5. At the start

EXAM QUESTION

a. catalysts
b. increases
c. decreases
d. reactants

pages 62–63
Energy
PROGRESS CHECK

1. Exothermic reaction
2. Endothermic
3. Energy

4. A reversible reaction
5. Endothermic

EXAM QUESTION

a. hydrated copper sulfate ↔ anhydrous copper sulfate + water
b. Changes colour from blue to white
c. Add it to white anhydrous copper sulphate and it would turn blue

pages 64–65
Aluminium
PROGRESS CHECK

1. Aluminium oxide
2. Cryolite
3. No
4. Yes
5. Aluminium

EXAM QUESTION

a. $Al^{3+} + 3e^- \rightarrow Al$
b. $2O^{2-} \rightarrow O_2 + 4e^-$
c. The oxygen that is produced reacts with the carbon electrode to make carbon dioxide

pages 66–67
Sodium Chloride
PROGRESS CHECK

1. The production of fertilisers; as colouring agents; in fireworks (any one)
2. Barium sulfate
3. barium chloride + sodium sulfate → barium sulfate + sodium chloride
4. Solid
5. Aqueous

EXAM QUESTION

a. Hydrogen
b. $2Cl^- \rightarrow Cl_2 + 2e^-$
c. To sterilise water

pages 68–69
Making Salts
PROGRESS CHECK

1. Neutral
2. Alkali
3. Acid

4. Magnesium chloride
5. Calcium chloride

EXAM QUESTION

a. calcium carbonate + hydrochloric acid → calcium chloride + water + carbon dioxide
b. Any number under 6 , but probably 1 or 2

Day 5

pages 70–71
Metals
PROGRESS CHECK

1. The attraction between positive metal ions and negative delocalised electrons
2. Alloys
3. Iron
4. Nickel
5. It turns limewater cloudy.

EXAM QUESTION

a. Steel
b. Brass

pages 72–73
Water
PROGRESS CHECK

1. Rock that contains water
2. To remove suspended particles like clay
3. To reduce levels of micro-organisms to acceptable levels
4. It uses a lot of energy
5. Nitrates

EXAM QUESTION

a. White precipitate
b. Silver chloride
c. Solid

pages 74–75
Detergents
PROGRESS CHECK

1. To remove stains
2. To remove stains at low temperatures
3. To make them more attractive
4. It helps the water to drain away

5. The maximum water temperature to use

EXAM QUESTION

a. To remove the dirt from the fabric
b. An acid
c. Hydrophilic end

pages 76–77
Special Materials
PROGRESS CHECK

1. Pencil lead; lubricant; electrodes (any one)
2. C_{60}
3. Fullerene, diamond and graphite
4. They are lustrous and colourless
5. Black

EXAM QUESTION

a. Each carbon atom is bonded to four others by strong covalent bonds
b. It has lots of strong covalent bonds
c. There are no free electrons/ions to move

pages 78–79
Vegetable Oils
PROGRESS CHECK

1. A and D
2. Sunflower oil; olive oil, corn oil, etc. (any two)
3. Seeds, nuts and fruits
4. They have carbon double bonds
5. One

EXAM QUESTION

a. Monosaturated
b. Polyunsaturated
c. Biofuel
d. Bromine water

pages 80–81
Alkanes and Alkenes
PROGRESS CHECK

1. C_nH_{2n+2}
2. Fuels
3. (covalent) bonds
4. Cracking

5. C_nH_{2n}

EXAM QUESTION

a. Alkenes
b. It has carbon double bonds
c. ethene + steam → ethanol

pages 82–83
Polymers
PROGRESS CHECK

1. Polypropene
2. It makes it more flexible
3. It will not soften but may eventually burn
4. They give off toxic gases
5. They are difficult to separate into the different types

EXAM QUESTION

a. Ethene
b. Alkenes
c. C_nH_{2n}

Day 6

pages 84–85
Motion
PROGRESS CHECK

1. Because they need to measure the distance travelled in a certain time
2. Average velocity = displacement / time
3. 20 m/s
4. Speed has magnitude (size) only; it is a **scalar** quantity. Velocity has magnitude and direction; it is a **vector** quantity.
5. Yes, because the direction changes

EXAM QUESTION

1. Acceleration = change in velocity / time taken
2. 5.0 m/s/s
3. 10 m/s/s
4. The velocity at two different points and the time between them

pages 86–87
Graphs for Motion
PROGRESS CHECK
1. The velocity
2. Greater velocity
3. The acceleration
4. The area under the graph
5. Negative acceleration (deceleration)

EXAM QUESTION

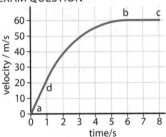

pages 88–89
When Forces Combine
PROGRESS CHECK
1. A free body diagram shows the forces that act on a single body
2.

3.
   400 N downwards
4. Because he pushes backwards on the boat in order to move forwards
5. Action – the man pushes backwards on the boat with a contact force. Reaction – the boat pushes forwards on the man with a contact force

EXAM QUESTION
a. No
b. They are not the same kind of force; they also act on the same body
c. The contact force of the girl

downwards on the bench (caused by the gravitational force of her weight)
d. A free body force diagram

pages 90–91
Forces and Motion
PROGRESS CHECK
1. 10 m/s/s
2. It would increase
3. A parachutist
4. Because it takes less velocity for the air resistance to balance the weight
5. Towards the centre

EXAM QUESTION
a. and b.

c. When the magnitude of the drag/air resistance equals the weight
d. Terminal velocity

pages 92–93
Momentum and Stopping
PROGRESS CHECK
1. 750 kgm/s
2. When a force acts on a body that is moving, or able to move, a change in momentum occurs
3. Where part of a car is designed to collapse steadily in a collision spreading stopping over longer time
4. The time it takes for a vehicle to stop
5. Greater stopping time means that less force is exerted on the passengers

EXAM QUESTION
a. 6.0 kgm/s
b. 3.0 kg
c. 6.0 kgm/s
d. 2.0 m/s

pages 94–95
Safe Driving
PROGRESS CHECK
1. The distance travelled between the need for braking occurring and the brakes starting to act
2. The distance taken to stop once the brakes have been applied
3. Driver tiredness; distractions; lack of concentration
4. If brakes are applied too hard the wheels will lock (stop turning) and the car will begin to skid. ABS braking systems detect this locking and automatically adjust the braking force to prevent skidding
5. Electric windows, cruise control, paddle shift controls on the steering wheel, adjustable seating

EXAM QUESTION
a. 50 m
b. 10 m
c. 5 m
d. Wet roads, speed

pages 96–97
Energy and Work
PROGRESS CHECK
1. Joules
2. kinetic energy = ½ × mass × velocity² / KE = ½ mv²
3. 9 J
4. Weight = mass × gravitational field strength
5. 45 N

EXAM QUESTION
a. Gravitational potential energy
b. 30 000 J
c. 30 000 J
d. 24 m/s

pages 98–99
Work and Power
PROGRESS CHECK
1. Work done is equal to energy transferred; work is done when a force moves an object
2. Joules
3. Climbing stairs, pulling a sledge (any reasonable answer)
4. 100 J
5. For an object that is able to recover its original shape, elastic potential is the energy stored in the object when work is done to change its shape

EXAM QUESTION
a. Gravity (his weight)
b. It is the distance moved in the direction of the force
c. 1000 J
d. No, he does the same

pages 100–101
Inside the Atom
PROGRESS CHECK
1. No charge, neutral
2. In an unstable nucleus a neutron may spontaneously change into a proton. When it does this, it emits an electron. This is called beta radiation
3. Huge distances
4. The ability of the radiation to cause other particles to gain or to lose electrons
5. Strong

EXAM QUESTION
a. Isotopes
b. 146
c. A helium nucleus (2 protons and 2 neutrons)
d. $^{238}_{92}U \rightarrow\ ^{234}_{90}Th + ^{4}_{2}\alpha$

Day 7

pages 102–103
Radiation and Science
PROGRESS CHECK
1. If a model is successfully tested,

scientists are more likely to accept it
2. Relativity
3. The electron
4. Because the electrons look a little bit like plums in a pudding
5. Electrons can behave like clouds of charge, or even waves.

EXAM QUESTION
a. Alpha particles
b. Because it is very thin
c. They passed straight through the gold foil
d. Most of an atom is empty space, most of the mass of an atom is compressed into a tiny volume in the centre called a nucleus, the nucleus of an atom has an overall positive charge

pages 104–105
Safe Radiation
PROGRESS CHECK
1. Rocks, cosmic rays and human use (e.g. medical)
2. Some media reports claim that it is
3. Because it can be breathed into the body
4. No
5. Yes

EXAM QUESTION
a. Fission
b. Risk of accidental emission of radioactive material; waste material disposal
c. The Earth's atmosphere and magnetic field and the ozone layer protects it
d. Use tongs or gloves, minimise the exposure time

pages 106–107
Nuclear Power
PROGRESS CHECK
1. Two lighter nuclei and two or three neutrons
2. The two lighter nuclei
3. It can be encased in glass or

concrete and buried
4. Thousands of years
5. The joining of two atomic nuclei to form a larger one

EXAM QUESTION
a. It slows down the neutrons (usually graphite or water)
b. They absorb some of the neutrons
c. No greenhouse gases; small amounts of fuel give large amounts of energy
d. High maintenance costs; risk of accidental emission of radioactive material

pages 108–109
Radiation Issues
PROGRESS CHECK
1. In fire alarms
2. To find leaks or blockages in underground pipes
3. To limit the exposure and therefore the damage to non-cancerous tissue
4. They are produced in different ways
5. X-rays are easier to control

EXAM QUESTION
1. The time it takes for the number of undecayed nuclei to halve
2. 3 days
3. 50 counts per second
4. The date of artefacts

pages 110–111
Static Electricity
PROGRESS CHECK
1. A material that charge (electrons) can pass through
2. A material that charge (electrons) cannot pass through
3. Aircraft fuel causes static charge as the fuel rubs against the pipe. A spark could ignite the fuel vapour. The aircraft and the tanker are earthed to avoid the charge building up
4. Correct earthing or use of

insulating mats
5. Synthetic clothing clings; dirt and dust are attracted to TV screens, etc; static shocks from cars, earthed conductors, etc. (any one)

EXAM QUESTION
a. Because each droplet repels the others, so they spread out evenly
b. No, the opposite charge
c. An even coat and less waste
d. In photocopiers

pages 112–113
Electricity on the Move 1
PROGRESS CHECK
1. Current is measured in Amps or Amperes – it is equal to the amount of charge that flows every second
2. a. True
   b. False, they flow from negative to positive
   c. False, ions do not move at all
   d. True

EXAM QUESTION
a., b. and c.

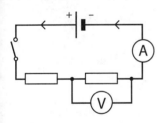

d. The current will stop flowing

pages 114–115
Electricity on the Move 2
PROGRESS CHECK
1. $1.5\,\Omega$
2. It will decrease.
3.

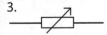

4. 4.1 A
5. 5.0 A

EXAM QUESTION
a. $10\,\Omega$
b. 1.2 A
c. 6.0 V
d. In parallel

pages 116–117
Using Electricity
PROGRESS CHECK
1.

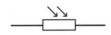

2. The resistance of a filament lamp increases with more current, the lamp gets hotter
3.

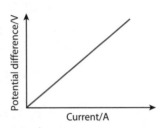

4. It increases
5. To detect high temperatures for a fire alarm

EXAM QUESTION
1. The fuse
2. The earth wire connects the metal parts of the hair dryer to earth and stops the device becoming dangerous to touch if there is a loose wire. If a large current flows to earth, the fuse melts and breaks the circuit
3. A residual current circuit breaker improves the safety of a device by disconnecting a circuit automatically whenever it detects that the flow of current is too high
4. The hairdryer is insulated with a plastic case and the wires themselves are also insulated

pages 118–119
Waves
PROGRESS CHECK
1. The distance between any point on a wave and the same point on the next wave
2. The maximum displacement of the waves from rest position
3. Longitudinal
4. Transverse
5. Yes, a.c. produces electricity that flows backwards and forwards, in a transverse wave shape

EXAM QUESTION
a. 30 000 Hz
b. To scan an image of an unborn baby; to look inside people's bodies; to measure speed of blood flow; to break down kidney stones (any one)
c. Does not damage living cells
d. It can produce images of soft tissue

Notes